THE Embellished Sock

THE EMBELLISHED SOCK

KNITTED ART FOR THE FOOT

CHARLES D. GANDY

ACORN CREEK PRESS

PUBLISHED BY

ACORN CREEK PRESS

PO Box 174
Clayton, Georgia 30525-0005

Copyright © 2012 by Charles D. Gandy

Photographs copyright © 2012 by
Peter McIntosh

All rights reserved. No part of this book may be reproduced or transmitted
in any form without prior written permission from the publisher.

1st printing, 2012

ISBN 978-0-9848012-0-6

Manufactured in Canada by Friesens Corporation

Edited by
Ava Navin

Book and cover design by
Burtch Hunter Design

CONTENTS

MY KNITTING JOURNEY 1
THE BASIC ANATOMY OF A SOCK 5

CARNIVAL 13
CELEBRATION 19
DREADSOX 25
FIESTA 31
FIRECRACKER 37
FIREFLY 43
JESTER 49
JULIE'S SOCK 55
LOOOOOOOOOPS 61
PEBBLES 67
RIPPLES 73
SNAKE IN THE GRASS 79
TILE SOCK 87
TIPTOE THRU THE TULIPS 93
TUBE SOCK 101
TWIST AND SHOUT 107
VARSITY 113
WINTER WONDERLAND 119

ABBREVIATIONS 124
RESOURCES 125
INDEX 127
ACKNOWLEDGMENTS 129

MY KNITTING JOURNEY

My mother, a knitwear designer and shop owner, taught me to knit when I was 4 or 5 years old. What a shock it was to go to school and learn that not every child knew how to knit. The inevitable childish kidding about my knitting soon ceased when the bullies realized that it didn't really matter to me what they said or thought. I liked to knit and enjoyed being able to do something that they couldn't. Thus my lifelong love of fiber began.

Afterschool hours were spent in Mother's shop. A simple place compared to today's standard, the shop carried one or two "good" yarn and needle brands and a few accessories. There were few, if any, novelty yarns and lots of straight needles, double points, and a few circular needles. Simple as it was, that shop was a wonderful place that provided a creative retreat for Momma's knitters.

While developing the various patterns for the socks in this book, I had to laugh when I used a plastic gadget to make the pompoms for the Fiesta Sock (featured on page 31). Pompom makers were certainly never on Momma's accessory wall. Instead, she taught me to make pompoms by cutting two circles of heavy cardstock with a large hole in the center. In those days we made lots of pompoms: pompoms for the cords that tied on baby hats, small pompoms for booties, big multicolored pompoms for the tops of ski caps. So there was lots of practice making those cardstock templates for pompoms. As nice as it is to have the new contraptions to help us, on page 35 you will find the instructions for making a pompom with the old-fashioned cardstock method.

Mother's knit shop was a great place to learn. I wound yarn, untangled impossibly snarled skeins, and ripped out mistakes ("frogging," as it is now called.) I even taught a few beginner classes and tried my hand at designing. I still have my first, somewhat bizarre and yet practical sweater designed at the age of seven. Momma, as do we all, had a ton of "stash." So I decided that if I made "half" sweaters that buttoned up the front *and* the back, we could use up that stash. That first sweater featured a "V" neck front and back with large buttons going up the front and, yes, down the back. The left side was gray, the right side was black, unless you used the third "half" and buttoned on the white side. Clever, no?

In college my fiber work shifted and expanded. As an Interior Design major, fiber-related courses were plentiful. I wove on 2-, 4-, and 8-harness looms. I dyed, batiked, and "shourbied" everything and anything. It was fun to experiment with knitting with heavy naval rope on needles fashioned from sharpened broomsticks and to explore working with plastic bags and tall grass and even dog hair. Life was good. And then my world fell apart . . . Mother, at the young age of 46, died.

Mourning my mother's death, I became determined to honor her legacy by making fiber a constant in my life. I created whimsical three-dimensional needlepoint fish that still adorn my walls. I wove large architectural wall hangings. And I continued to knit: an occasional sweater, a random pair of socks, a vest, a cap. All were done with joy and gratitude for my mother's dedication to teaching a young boy to knit.

After the tragic events of September 11, 2001, I decided to leave my successful interior design practice and live a simpler, quieter life. It was then that my knitting became an obsession. My stash began to grow. My collection of needles, accessories and gadgets expanded. And after many years, I decided to make a pair of socks. The "self-striping" yarns that imitate Fair Isle patterns fascinated me. Turning a heel with short rows and picking up stitches to make a gusset excited me. Ann Budd's book, *Getting Started Knitting Socks,* helped me to thoroughly understand the architecture of a sock. Cat Bordhi's ingenious sock designs and construction stimulated my creativity. I was enthralled with making socks. Everyone I knew got a new pair of socks, whether they wanted them or not.

Every Sunday afternoon my friends and I usually gather at our local café, Grapes & Beans, to knit, talk politics, and enjoy good food. At one such gathering in the fall of 2008, I was thumbing through a new issue of Knitter's Magazine, and an ad for their "Think Outside the Sox" contest caught my eye. Having always loved contests, I immediately downloaded the entry information and began thinking about socks . . . socks! Socks! Various manufacturers sponsored numerous ingenious categories, each very specific about which yarn to feature and what they were expecting. With a limit of only five pairs of socks per knitter, I studied those categories carefully, eliminating some and circling others. My mind was spinning with ideas. The contest had been announced in the spring, and it was now fall. With the deadline the end of December, I had to get to work. Some ideas came quickly. DreadSox (featured on page 25) is a good example. Regia, one of the sponsors, wanted socks to be worn with sandals. I thought the simple dramatic strength of the dreads would appeal to the judges, and I was fascinated to explore what would happen when I changed the intended diameter of Regia's self-striping yarn.

I worked hard on those contest socks, creating new techniques in the process: for example, the detail for knitting in the I-cords on the Dreadsox. I remembered making finger cords as a child and knew they would be perfect for the Snake in the Grass sock (featured on page 79). I went to my local yarn shops and searched for the various yarns specified in the competition. I sketched, dreamed, and experimented with sample after sample, eventually making five pairs of socks in three months, spending three full weeks for just the Snake in the Grass socks. I sent the socks off and waited for the results. Finally the announcement came. I WON . . . not in one category . . . but TWO: for DreadSox and Snake in the Grass. Wow! The judges liked my socks. What fun it had been making them and how gratifying to learn that other knitters—professional knitters—appreciated them.

In the fall of 2009, almost a year after the competition, I went to a workshop led by Cat Bordhi, a judge in the contest. She complimented my work and told me of her "visionary" workshops, where she invited expert knitters to work with her and learn how to publish their work. She sent me an application for a "men only" retreat that she was planning for March 2010.

Part of that application was to propose a book. But what kind of book? I questioned if my patterns for knitted toys would make a good book. Or should I write about my interest in various dyeing techniques? Then it hit me that I needed to write about what I knew best . . . socks! But another sock book? Does the knitting world really need another sock book? What would set my book apart from all the others? As I pondered that question, in preparation to apply for the Men's Visionary Workshop, it became clear that what sets my socks apart is their embellishment. Numerous books already on the market explain how to make a basic sock. Scores of other books explore various patterns, from lace to cables to ribbing, but few, if any, delve into the world of embellishment.

Luckily, Cat accepted my proposal and invited me to join nine other knitters . . . all men! What a life-changing experience for us all. I remember, as I began to present my ideas to the group, thinking that these talented guys were going to laugh me out of the room. Well, to my surprise and relief, they not only didn't laugh at me, they congratulated me. Being conscious that the inside of any knitted garment should look as good as or better than the outside, I have struggled with various ways to make the finished product better. According to my fellow "visionaries," my efforts paid off, as they complimented me on the insides of my socks and encouraged me to explain my finishing techniques and explore more. In addition, the group helped me expand my vision, offering the subtitle of the book "Knitted Art for the Foot." The retreat changed my life. Thank you, guys. Thank you, Cat.

So my knitting journey, as I am sure for many of you, has been a life-long pursuit. My hope is that, as you knit these socks and as you use these techniques to create your own visions, you will join me in honoring the person who taught you this great tradition we call knitting. For me, of course, it is my Mother.

C. D. G.

THE BASIC ANATOMY OF A SOCK

For many knitters, there seems to be an unexplainable mystery around knitting a sock. Many think it is just too complicated for them to tackle. Others marvel when they see someone knitting a sock without using a pattern. Socks are fun to make. They offer just enough challenge and technique to make them intriguing, and at the same time they provide a blank canvas upon which the knitter may create an individual statement.

Understanding the basic anatomy of a sock takes away the mystery and opens the doors to untold hours of creative knitting.

For the most part, socks are knitted from the top down or from the toes up. A few creative designers have ventured beyond the norm and make their socks from the heel out or from other unusual points. This book presents patterns that are worked from the top down. Likewise, these patterns call for double point needles. If you are more comfortable using two circular needles or the technique known as Magic Loop . . . then go for it. The number of stitches is the same, the anatomy is the same. It is just a matter of personal preference. For the socks in this book, there are seven basic sections: TOP, LEG, HEEL FLAP, HEEL TURN, GUSSET, FOOT and TOE. Thoroughly understanding the characteristics of and options for each of these sections will make knitting the sock more enjoyable and will eventually lead to being able to make a sock without a pattern at all.

TOP

It is convenient to remember that an average adult leg is approximately 8 inches in circumference. Of course, a smaller size would be slightly smaller and larger sizes correspondingly larger. Knowing this number, multiplied by your gauge, will give you a key number that will help you remember all the various stages of the sock. Let's assume you are casting on 64 stitches . . . the "key" number. Using four double point needles (3 needles for the stitches and 1 as a working needle) cast on ¼ the key number (16 stitches) on needle #1, ½ the key number (32) stitches on needle #2, (these stitches will be the front of the leg and the instep of the sock) and the final ¼ on needle #3. Placing the stitches on the needle like this becomes a "marker," with each round beginning on needle #1. This position on the needles will be the back center of the leg of the sock throughout.

There are several options for how to handle the top of a sock. The final decision, of course, depends on the desired look of the finished sock. Traditionally, socks are ribbed at the top. There is no "standard" for this ribbing. Anything will work, from K1, P1, K2, P2, and any variation of that theme. The length of the ribbing is dependent on the overall length of the leg and should therefore be proportional to the overall look of the sock. Ribbing, however, isn't the only approach to the top of a sock. A hemmed edge is a very plausible option. A simple purl round at the turn on the hem is an easy way to make a nice finished edge of such a top. Or for more detail, a picot edge is a very simple, yet beautiful, way to begin a sock. Even within a hemmed approach there are options: sewing the hem into place after the sock is finished, or casting on with a provisional cast-on and then knitting the basic hem, removing the waste yarn, and then attaching the hem by knitting two stitches together around. This provisional cast-on approach provides a beautiful finished detail. Whether to sew or knit in the hem depends on the final design of the sock and what may or may not need to take place at the hem. Let the design suggest the solution.

LEG

The length of the leg plus the top depends on the desired finished look and design of the sock. As a rule, that length will be approximately 7½ inches, plus or minus. For most socks, the leg of the sock is a simple tube that covers the desired length of the leg. It is in this section that creativity can abound. From something as easy as simple striping to covering the leg with a multitude of bobbles or beads, the leg of the sock is a great place to express your creativity.

HEEL FLAP

Self-describing, the heel flap is the section of the sock that falls just below the leg and at the back of the heel and is worked on half the total key stitches. (Combine the stitches on needle #1 and those on needle #3). Because the heel flap will receive as much or more wear than any other part of the sock, it should be knitted with a dense stitch pattern to help ensure durability. For this book, the heel flap is worked with a slip 1, knit 1 detail on the right-side row and then slipping the first stitch on the purl row and purling across. That simple detail provides just enough texture and density to the heel flap to make it durable. There are a number of variations on this technique: alternating the slip stitches: working a seed stitch, a ribbing, and many other textured stitch patterns. Just remember, as a rule, the heel flap is approximately a square, so an easy way to make sure it is long enough is to simply fold your work over diagonally. If the row with slipped stitches at the top of the needle aligns with the first row of the heel flap, you are probably where you need to be.

HEEL TURN

Sometimes called "short rows," this section of the sock provides an intriguing shaping for the heel . . . it turns the corner, so to speak. Worked on the stitches of the heel flap, the technique is simple and easy to remember without a pattern. The first row is worked in stockinette until 2 stitches beyond the center stitch (18). Then the first of several decreases is made, followed by working a single stitch. The work is then turned, the first stitch slipped, working 5 stitches, decreasing and then purling a single stitch. And turn again . . . thus the short row . . . you have only worked across a short portion of the total row. This process continues by knitting a short row, decreasing, turning and repeating until all the stitches have been worked and the heel is shaped. This technique allows the knitter to basically "sculpt" the heel and is always fascinating to do.

GUSSET

In preparation for making the gusset and in an effort to learn to make socks without a pattern, knit ½ the remaining stitches of the short rows. (9: ½ of 18). With a new needle, which will now be needle #1, knit the remaining stitches (9). You will now be ready to pick up stitches along either side of the heel flap for the gusset. Picking up these stitches, if it is done correctly, will make the sock appear handmade, not homemade. Careful attention should be paid as you pick up these stitches, making sure that they are even and are picked up in the exact same manner along the way. (The slipped stitch at the beginning of every row of the heel flap provides a guideline for picking up these stitches.) Picking up the stitches along this edge is a cause for much angst for many knitters. Most patterns will specify the exact number of stitches that need to be

picked up along the edge. Instead of concentrating on this exact number, a better approach is to allow the knitting itself to tell you how many stitches to pick up. Making sure that stitches are plentiful in the corners of the gusset will help ensure that no holes will be exposed. It is also good to remember that there is no need to fret if the number of stitches on either side of the gusset is different, as long as there are no more than, say, two extra stitches. Those stitches can be taken care of in the first few decrease rows of the gusset. Once you have picked up the stitches along the first edge of the gusset, all done on needle #1, change to needle #2 and work the instep stitches (32). Then, with needle #3, pick up the stitches for the opposite side of the gusset and finish by knitting the original stitches (½ the key number) from the heel flap. As the gusset is worked, another detail that separates *good* sock knitters from *better* sock knitters is to make the decreases at the base of the gusset and just before the instep mirror one another. So if the decrease at the beginning of the gusset is a K2tog that leans to the right, then the decrease on the other side should be an SSK that leans to the left. It's those details that make the difference. To work without a pattern, just remember that you decrease on one round and not on the second round, and only on the gusset stitches, leaving the instep stitches the same, and that you continue until you have decreased to the original number of stitches as on the leg. (16 sts on needle #1, 32 on needle #2, and 16 on needle #3.)

FOOT

The foot is another tube that works its way down to the toe. In working this section of the sock, remember that it will be inside the shoe and therefore shouldn't be too bulky or patterned to interfere with comfort. The bottom of the sock should, in most cases, be worked in a stockinette stitch, while the instep or top of the foot may be worked in a simple, unobtrusive pattern. As a general rule of thumb, the length of the foot will be measured 2 inches short of the finished length of the sock (just at the base of the toe), measuring from the back of the heel. For my own personal socks, that number is 7 ½ inches . . . the same as the length of the leg.

TOE

There are two toe options: a standard toe which follows the shape of the toe, or a tabi (flip-flop) toe. Both are easy to accomplish. The standard toe decreases one stitch on either side of the foot, on both the sole side and the instep side, on every other row until half the stitches remain (8 on needles #1 and 3 and 16 on needle #2) and then on *every* row until 8 stitches remain. These stitches are then grafted by using the Kitchener stitch. (See page 41) The tabi toe is worked, like a mitten, with a left and right. The stitches to work the big toe section are held separately from the stitches for the other toes. Again, the sock is finished with the Kitchener stitch.

Once all the knitting is done, carefully work in all ends and finish according to the directions, block and enjoy wearing!

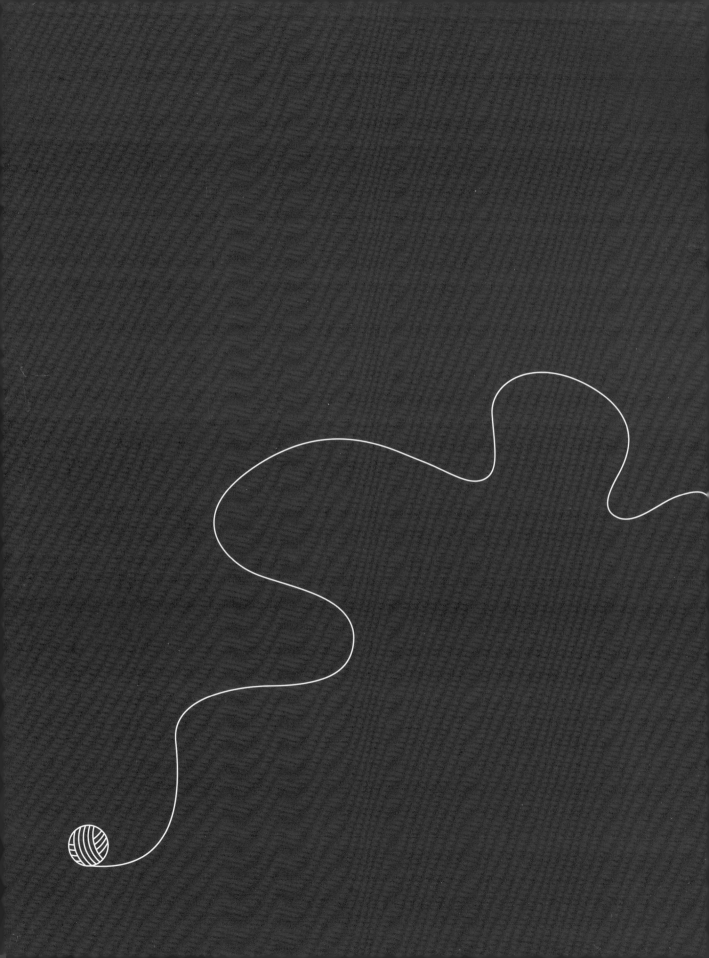

THE Embellished Sock

KNITTED ART FOR THE FOOT

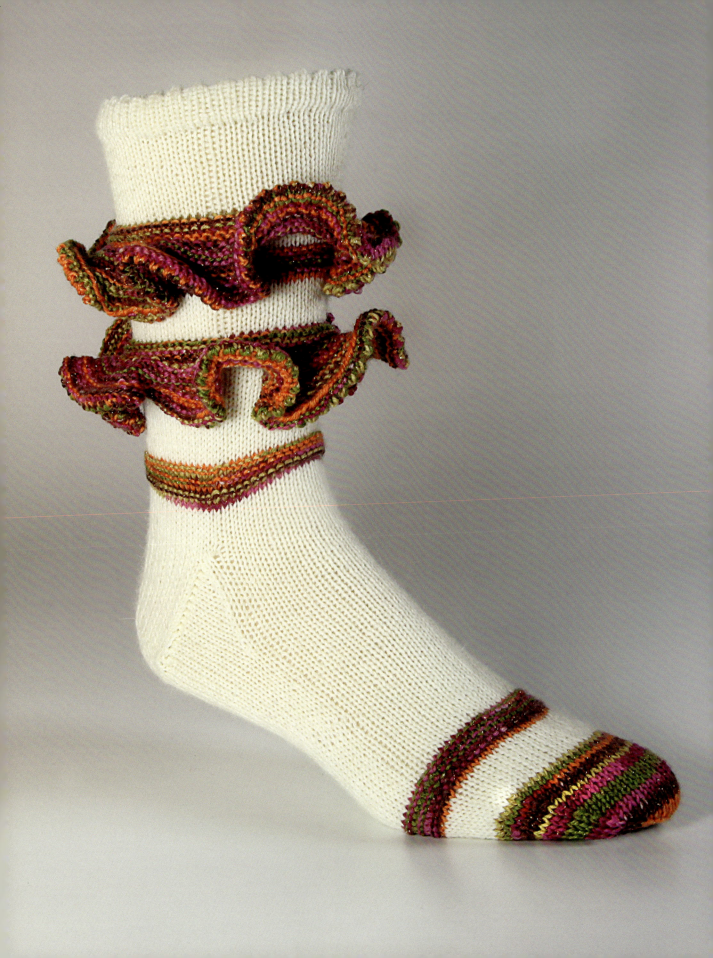

CARNIVAL

For me, making ruffles is one of the special pleasures of knitting. The simplicity of dramatically increasing (or decreasing!) in a short distance of your work, causing the fabric to ruffle, is always fun. For this double-ruffle sock, using a glittery metallic yarn, I added a special picot edge for a bit of extra detail. This is one of those socks that is easy to adapt. Experiment with different colors for the ruffles. Consider adding stripes along the way. Or what about adding a third or fourth ruffle? ¡Olé!

SIZES CM: 6" (CL: 7", AS: 8", AM: 9", AL: 10") leg circumference

GAUGE 8 stitches per inch

YARN Fingering Weight
For socks: (MC):
> 1 Skein (400-425 yds) Berroco, Ultra Alpaca Fine, #1201 Winter White
> 50% Wool, 20% Super Fine Alpaca, 30% Nylon

For Ruffles: (CC):
> 1 Skein (380 yds) Berroco, Sox Metallic, #1375 Guava
> 73% Superwash Wool, 25% Nylon, 2% Other Fibers

Waste yarn for provisional cast-on (optional)

NEEDLES Two sets of DPN size 1 (2.25 mm), or size to obtain gauge
Two 16" size 1 (2.25 mm) circular, or size to obtain gauge

NOTIONS Tapestry needle
Markers (optional)
Size C (2.75 mm) crochet hook for provisional cast-on (optional)

TO MAKE RUFFLES

Make 4 pieces in CC color (2 for each sock). (I found it easier to make one ruffle and leave it on the second pair of DPNs, then knit the sock until you are ready to attach the ruffle. Then, once the extra needles are free, knit the second ruffle.)

For the edge of this Ruffle you have two options: a knitted-in hem where you use a Provisional Cast-On, or a Turned Edge where you do a regular cast-on and hem when finished.

Provisional Cast-On (See page 105): Using the waste yarn and a circular needle, CO 192 (224, 256, 288, 320).

Turned Edge: Using a circular needle CO 192 (224, 256, 288, 320) sts.

For either cast-on, join, being careful not to twist.

Place a marker to mark the beginning of the round and work in garter stitch (K 1 round, P 1 round) for 4 rounds, forming 2 garter-stitch ridges.

Round 4: Picot edge: *K2tog, YO, repeat from * around.

Work in garter stitch for 4 more rounds, beginning with a knit round.

If you chose the Provisional Cast-On, remove the waste yarn and retrieve the stitches on the second circular needle. Fold at the picot edge. Carefully match the first stitch of the front needle to the first stitch of the back needle, and k2tog around to "hem" the picot edge.

Work in garter stitch for 7 rounds, beginning with a purl round.

Round 17: Change to DPNs. K2tog around, placing 12 (14, 16, 18, 20) sts on needle #1, 24 (28, 32, 36, 40) sts on needle #2, and 12 (14, 16, 18, 20) sts on needle #3, for a total of 48 (56, 64, 72, 80) sts.

Work in garter stitch for 5 rounds, beginning with a purl round.

Cut yarn, leaving a 6" tail. Leave the ruffle on the DPNs. Put aside to await the attachment round.

LEG

For the edge of this sock you have two options: a knitted-in hem where you use a Provisional Cast-On, or a Turned Edge where you do a regular cast-on and hem when finished.

Provisional Cast-On (See page 105): Using waste yarn, CO 48 (56, 64, 72, 80) sts, distributed onto DPNs as follows:

> Needle #1: 12 (14, 16, 18, 20)
> Needle #2: 24 (28, 32, 36, 40)
> Needle #3: 12 (14, 16, 18, 20)

Join, being careful not to twist.

K 8 rounds, work a picot edge (K2tog, YO around), K 8 more rounds, remove the provisional cast-on, place the stitches on DPNs and then, using a third needle, k2tog around, taking one st from the front needle and one from the back needle. Thus, you will have a neat, finished hem.

Turned Edge: Using MC, CO 48 (56, 64, 72, 80) sts, distributed onto DPNs as follows:

> Needle #1: 12 (14, 16, 18, 20)
> Needle #2: 24 (28, 32, 36, 40)
> Needle #3: 12 (14, 16, 18, 20)

Join, being careful not to twist.

Knit 8 rounds. (These rounds will be turned to form a hem during the finishing process.)

For Picot Edge: *K2tog, YO. Repeat from * around.

For either cast-on, knit until piece measures 2" from picot edge, ending with needle #3.

Add Ruffle: Hold DPN #1 of the ruffle on top of and parallel with needle #1 of the sock leg. Using MC, *k2tog, taking the first st from the ruffle needle and the second st from the leg needle. Repeat from * across each needle, thus attaching the ruffle to the leg.

K 7 rounds.

Cut yarn, leaving a 6" tail. Change to CC.

THREE-NEEDLE ATTACHMENT

Place the piece to be attached in front of the left-hand needle, right sides facing. Knit 2 together, picking up one stitch from the front needle and one from the back needle. Work across attachment.

For video instructions please visit:
www.youtube.com/watch?v=tdwBWmLm1Zg

Round 1 Knit.

Round 2 With yarn in back, Sl 1 purlwise, then P to end of round. (Slipping this first stitch here and at each color change will avoid the "jog" at the color change.)

Work in garter stitch for 5 rounds, beginning with a knit round.

Change to MC and K 8 rounds.

Make second ruffle and attach as above.

K for 2" from second ruffle.

Change to CC. Beginning with a knit round, work in garter stitch for 7 rounds, remembering to slip the first stitch of the second round.

Change to MC and K 8 rounds, ending on needle #2.

Using the three-needle attachment for the ruffles, the inside of the sock is uninterrupted.

HEEL FLAP

Beginning on needle #3 (RS), *Sl 1 as if to P, K 1, repeat from *, working across needles 3 and 1. You now have a total of 24 (28, 32, 36, 40) sts on each of the 2 needles. (The stitches held on needle #2 will be worked later for the instep.)

Row 1 Turn work (WS). Sl 1 purlwise, P to end of row.

Row 2 Turn work (RS). *Sl 1 purlwise, K 1, repeat from * across row.

Repeat Rows 1 and 2 for a total of 24 (28, 32, 36, 40) rows, ending with row 1.

TURNING THE HEEL (Short Rows)

Row 1 (RS) K 14 (16, 18, 20, 22), SSK, K 1, turn work.

Row 2 (WS) Sl 1 purlwise, P5, P2tog, P 1, turn work.

Row 3 Sl 1 purlwise, K until 1 st before the gap formed on last row, SSK (bringing together the st before and the st after the gap). K 1. Turn work.

Row 4 Sl 1 purlwise, P until 1 st before the gap formed on last row, P2tog (1 st before the gap and 1 st after the gap), P 1. Turn work.

Repeat rows 3 and 4 until all sts have been worked, ending on row 4 (WS). In some sizes the last 2 rows may not have a single stitch to knit or purl, so end those 2 rows with the decrease of SSK or P2tog. You will have 14 (16, 18, 20, 22) sts remaining.

GUSSET

Working on the heel flap, K 7 (8, 9, 10, 11) sts. With a new needle (which becomes needle #1), K 7 (8, 9, 10, 11) sts. On the same needle, pick up 12-14 (14-16, 16-18, 18-20, 20-22) sts along the side of the heel flap.

Work across needle #2 (the instep stitches that have been waiting patiently). For needle #3, pick up 12-14 (14-16, 16-18, 18-20, 20-22) sts from the other side of the heel flap, and then K the 7 (8, 9, 10, 11) sts from the heel flap. You should now have (more or less) 20 (23, 26, 29, 32) on needle #1, 24 (28, 32, 36, 40) sts on needle #2, and 20 (23, 26, 29, 32) on needle #3.

Round 1 Needle #1, K until 3 sts remain, K2tog, K 1. On needle #2, K across. On needle #3, K 1, SSK, K to end.

> This first decrease round is a good chance to take care of that extra stitch that you may have picked up along one side of your heel flap. For example, if you have 23 sts on needle #1 and 22 sts on needle #3, do the decrease on needle #1 and omit it on needle #3 for one round only. Then you will have an equal number of stitches on both sides of your heel flap.

Round 2 Knit.

Repeat Rounds 1 and 2 until you have 12 (14, 16, 18, 20) sts on needle #1, 24 (28, 32, 36, 40) on needle #2, and 12 (14, 16, 18, 20) on needle #3.

> You have shaped your heel and returned to the same number of stitches you cast on.

FOOT

Knit until piece measures 4½" (5½", 6½", 7½", 8") from the back of the heel to the base of the big toe, approximately 3" shorter than the desired finished size.

Change to CC. Beginning with a knit round, work in garter stitch for 7 rounds, remembering to slip the first stitch of the second round to avoid the "jog" at the color change.

Change to main color and K 8 rounds.

Change to CC and K 1 round, remembering to slip the first stitch of the second round.

TOE

Round 1

> Needle #1: work until 3 sts remain, K2tog, K 1.
> Needle #2: K 1, SSK, K until 3 sts remain, K2tog, K 1.
> Needle #3: K 1, SSK, K to end.

Round 2 Knit.

Repeat Rounds 1 and 2 until 5 (7, 8, 9, 10) sts remain on needle #1, 10 (14, 16, 18, 20) sts on needle #2, and 5 (7, 8, 9,10) sts on needle #3.

Then repeat Round 1 until a total of 8 sts remain (4 sts on 2 needles).

Graft these 8 sts by using Kitchener stitch. (See page 41)

FINISHING

If you chose the Turned Edge option for the sock top and/or the ruffles, turn at the picot edge and hem carefully.

Work in all loose ends.

CELEBRATION

Have you met a yarn that talked to you? Well this sock resulted after just such a "conversation." While on a visit to my local yarn shop, the classic pastel colors of this yarn called out to me, "Make me into a party sock!" The bands of reverse stockinette stitch might be interpreted as icing flowing from the layers of cake, while the finger cords, complete with the tiny ties for flames, remind me of glowing birthday candles. These elements all work together to make the sock come to life and sparkle. Party away!

SIZES CM: 6" (CL: 7", AS: 8", AM: 9", AL: 10") leg circumference

GAUGE 6 stitches per inch

YARN DK Weight

Color A: 4 Skeins (400-425 yds) Sublime, Bamboo & Pearls DK, #K014-215
70% Bamboo Sourced Viscose, 30% Pearl Sourced Viscose

Color B: 6-8 yards Sublime, Bamboo & Pearls DK, #K014-211
70% Bamboo Sourced Viscose, 30% Pearl Sourced Viscose

Color C: 6-8 yards Sublime, Bamboo & Pearls DK, #K014-212
70% Bamboo Sourced Viscose, 30% Pearl Sourced Viscose

Color D: 6-8 yards Sublime, Bamboo & Pearls DK, #K014-210
70% Bamboo Sourced Viscose, 30% Pearl Sourced Viscose

Color E: 6-8 yards Sublime, Bamboo & Pearls DK, #K014-208
70% Bamboo Sourced Viscose, 30% Pearl Sourced Viscose

Color F: 6-8 yards Sublime, Bamboo & Pearls DK, #K014-214
70% Bamboo Sourced Viscose, 30% Pearl Sourced Viscose

NEEDLES DPN size 4 (3.50 mm), or size to obtain gauge

NOTIONS Tapestry needle
Markers (optional)

LEG

Using Color A, CO 36 (40, 48, 52, 60) sts, as follows:

Needle #1: 9 (10, 12, 13, 15)
Needle #2: 18 (20, 24, 26, 30)
Needle #3: 9 (10, 12, 13, 15)

Join, being careful not to twist.

Knit 6 rounds.

Change to color B and K 1 round.

For a "jogless" stripe here and at each color change, slip first stitch of second round.

Purl 3 rounds.

Change to color A and K 5 (7, 9, 10, 11) rounds.

Change to color C and K 1 round, then P 3 rounds.

Change to color A and K 5 (7, 9, 10, 11) rounds.

Change to color D and K 1 round, then P 3 rounds.

Change to color A and K 5 (7, 9, 10, 11) rounds.

Change to color E and K 1 round, then P 3 rounds.

Change to color A and K 5 (7, 9, 10, 11) rounds.

Change to color F and K 1 round, then P 3 rounds.

Change to color A and K until piece measures 5½" (6½", 7½", 8½", 9½"), ending with the last st on needle #2.

HEEL FLAP

Beginning on needle #3 (RS), * Sl 1 purlwise, K 1, repeat from *, working across needles 3 and 1. You now have a total of 18 (20, 24, 26, 30) sts on each of the 2 needles. (The stitches held on needle #2 will be worked later for instep.)

Row 1 Turn work (WS). Sl 1 purlwise, P to end of row.

Row 2 Turn work (RS). *Sl 1 purlwise, K 1, repeat from * across row.

Repeat Rows 1 and 2 for a total of 20 (22, 24, 26, 28) rows, ending with row 1.

TURNING THE HEEL (Short Rows)

Row 1 (RS) K 11 (12, 14, 15, 17), SSK, K 1, turn work.

Row 2 (WS) Sl 1 purlwise, P 5, P2tog, P 1, turn work.

Row 3 Sl 1 purlwise, K until 1 st before the gap formed on last row, SSK (bringing together the st before the gap and the st after the gap). K 1. Turn work.

Row 4 Sl 1 purlwise, P until 1 st before the gap formed on last row, P2tog (1 st before the gap and 1 st after the gap), P 1. Turn work.

Repeat rows 3 and 4 until all sts have been worked, ending on row 4 (WS). In some sizes the last 2 rows may not have a single stitch to knit or purl, so end those 2 rows with the decrease of SSK or P2tog. You will have 12 (12, 14, 16, 18) sts remaining.

GUSSET

Working on the heel flap, K 6 (6, 7, 8, 9) sts. With a new needle (which becomes needle #1), K 6 (6, 7, 8, 9) sts. On same needle, pick up and K 10-12 (11-13, 12-14, 13-15, 14-16) sts along the side of the heel flap.

Work across needle #2 (the instep stitches that have been waiting patiently). For needle #3, pick up and K 10-12 (11-13, 12-14, 13-15, 14-16) sts from the other side of the heel flap, and then K the 6 (6, 7, 8, 9) sts from the heel flap. You should now have (more or less) 17 (18, 20, 22, 24) sts on needle #1, 18 (20, 24, 26, 30) sts on needle #2, and 17 (18, 20, 22, 24) on needle #3.

Round 1 Needle #1, K until 3 sts remain, K2tog, K 1. On needle #2, K across. On needle #3, K 1, SSK, K to end.

> This first decrease round is a good chance to take care of that extra stitch that you may have picked up along one side of your heel flap. For example, if you have 22 sts on needle #1 and 23 sts on needle #3, do the decrease on needle #1 and omit it on needle #3 for one time only. Thus, you will have an even number of stitches on both sides of your heel flap.

Round 2 Knit.

Repeat Rounds 1 and 2 until you have 9 (10, 12, 13, 15) sts on needle #1, 18 (20, 24, 26, 30) on needle #2, and 9 (10, 12, 13, 15) on needle #3.

> You have shaped your heel and returned to the same number of stitches you cast on.

FOOT

Work until piece measures 5½" (6½", 7½", 8½", 9") from the back of the heel to the base of the big toe, approximately 2" shorter than the desired finished size.

TOE

Round 1

Needle #1: work until 3 sts remain, K2tog, K 1.
Needle #2: K 1, SSK, K until 3 sts remain, K2tog, K 1.
Needle #3: K 1, SSK, K to end.

Round 2 Knit.

Repeat Rounds 1 and 2 until 5 (7, 8, 9, 10) sts remain on needle #1, 10 (14, 16, 18, 20) sts on needle #2, and 5 (7, 8, 9, 10) sts on needle #3.

Then repeat Round 1 until a total of 8 sts remain (4 sts on 2 needles).

Graft these 8 sts by using Kitchener stitch. (See page 41)

FINISHING

Using color A in 24" lengths, make 50 (60, 80, 90, 100) finger cords for each sock. (See opposite page)

Using a tapestry needle, securely attach each finger cord at the base of the purl bands, going into one stitch, pulling the ends to the back and tying a square knot. Repeat around the leg, attaching a finger cord to every 3rd (4th, 3rd, 4th, 3rd) stitch.

For accent, thread yarn the color of the corresponding stripe through the end of each cord. Tie securely with a square knot, and then trim to about ¼".

Turn at the purl edge and hem for a neat cuff.

Work in any loose ends.

FINGER CORDS

For these projects, the finger cords are all made of a solid color. But for learning purposes, two colors have been used to show how the same "side" of the yarn stays in the same hand throughout the length of the cord. To make the cord of a solid color, fold a length of yarn in half and make a slip knot, then proceed as follows:

1 Make a slip knot (in red) in the middle of the yarn and place this knot between your middle finger and your thumb of your right hand. Extend a loop (red) with your right index finger.

2 Holding the yellow yarn in your left hand, extend your left index finger, going over and into the red loop on your right finger. (Do NOT wrap the yellow yarn around your left index finger . . . a common mistake!)

3 Pick up a new loop (yellow) with your left index finger and extend a loop.

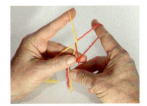

4 Transfer the slipknot from your right hand to the middle finger and thumb of your left hand. Release the red loop from the right index finger and gently but snugly tighten the red loop.

5 Repeat #3 and #4 with your right hand picking up a LOOP with the red yarn. Again, TRANSFER the knot to your middle index finger of your right hand. COVER the knot with your right thumb. RELEASE the yellow loop and PULL it gently but firmly.

6 Repeat the process: Loop, Transfer, Cover, Release, and Pull, going from one hand (and loop) to the other until you reach the desired length. To bind off, simply pull the yarn through the last loop.

For video instructions please visit:
www.youtube.com/watch?v=HDvUp3gefmM

DREADSOX

When I learned of Knitter's Magazine's and XRX Inc.'s "Think Outside the Sox" contest, I was hooked. There is nothing like a competition to get the creative juices flowing. One of the sponsors, Regia, asked for a sock to be worn with crocs, sandals, or Uggs! Something three-dimensional seemed the best solution. Working with my career-long concept of "simplify and then exaggerate," I thought of using the simple I-cord . . . but not just a few: tons of I-cords. I worked on numerous samples to find an effective way to "knit-in" the I-cords. Working with Regia's 6-Ply Square color, a self-striping yarn, also intrigued me. What would happen when I used this special yarn on the smaller diameter of the I-cord instead of on the leg of a sock as it was designed? As I suspected it would, the stripe became a solid in the smaller diameter. Featuring scores of "dreads" on each sock, the DreadSox won in its category. These socks are fun to make and even more fun to wear.

SIZES	CM: 6" (CL: 7", AS: 8", AM: 9", AL: 10") leg circumference
GAUGE	6 stitches per inch

YARN	DK Weight
	MC: 3 Skeins (400-425 yds) Regia, 6 Ply #540
	    75% Superwash Wool, 25% Polyamide
	CC: 3 Skeins (400-425 yds) Regia, 6 Ply Square, Color #1126
	    75% Superwash Wool, 25% Polyamide

NEEDLES	DPN size 4 (3.5 mm), or size to obtain gauge
NOTIONS	Tapestry needle Markers (optional) 90 (100, 120, 135, 150) Coilless safety pins or small stitch holders Two strips of ¼" elastic, cut to fit the calf of the leg Sewing thread

LEG

Using MC, CO 36 (40, 48, 52, 60) sts, distributed onto DPNs as follows:

    Needle #1: 9 (10, 12, 13, 15)
    Needle #2: 18 (20 24, 26, 30)
    Needle #3: 9 (10, 12, 13, 15)

Join, being careful not to twist.

Knit 10 rounds (to form a Rev St St roll when finished.)

Round 11 * K2, slip 2 sts onto a safety pin or holder. Using the backward loop method, CO 2 sts. Repeat from * around. (See page 29)

Round 12, 13 Knit.

Round 14 *Slip 2 sts onto a holder. Using the backward loop method, CO 2 sts, K2. Repeat from * around.

Rounds 15, 16 Knit.

Round 17 Repeat Round 11.

Rounds 18, 19 Knit.

Round 20 Repeat round 14.

Rounds 21, 22 Knit.

Round 23 Repeat Round 11.

Knit every round until piece measures 6" (7", 8", 9", 9½"), ending with the last st on needle #2.

HEEL FLAP

Beginning on needle #3 (RS), * Sl 1 purlwise, K 1, repeat from *, working across needles 3 and 1. You now have a total of 18 (20, 24, 26, 30) sts on each of the 2 needles. (The stitches held on needle #2 will be worked later for instep.)

Row 1 Turn work (WS). Sl 1 purlwise, P to end of row.

Row 2 Turn work (RS). *Sl 1 purlwise, K 1, repeat from * across row.

Repeat Rows 1 and 2 for a total of 20 (22, 24, 26, 28) rows, ending with row 1.

TURNING THE HEEL (Short Rows)

Row 1 (RS) Knit 11 (12, 14, 15, 17), SSK, K 1, turn work.

Row 2 (WS) Sl 1 purlwise, P 5, P2tog, P 1, turn work.

Row 3 Sl 1 purlwise, K until 1 st before the gap formed on last row, SSK (bringing together the st before the gap and the st after the gap). K 1. Turn work.

Row 4 Sl 1 purlwise, P until 1 st before the gap formed on last row, P2tog (1 st before the gap and 1 st after the gap), P 1. Turn work.

Repeat rows 3 and 4 until all sts have been worked, ending on row 4 (WS). In some sizes the last 2 rows may not have a single stitch to knit or purl, so end those 2 rows with the decrease of SSK or P2tog. You will have 12 (12, 14, 16, 18) sts remaining.

GUSSET

Working on the heel flap, K 6 (6, 7, 8, 9) sts. With a new needle (which becomes needle #1), K 6 (6, 7, 8, 9) sts. On the same needle, pick up and K 10-12 (11-13, 12-14, 13-15, 14-16) sts along the side of the heel flap.

Work across needle #2 (the instep stitches that have been waiting patiently). For needle #3, pick up and K 10-12 (11-13, 12-14, 13-15, 14-16) sts from the other side of the heel flap, and then K the 6 (6, 7, 8, 9) sts from the heel flap. You should now have (more or less) 17 (18, 20, 22, 24) on needle #1, 18 (20, 24, 26, 30) sts on needle #2, and 17 (18, 20, 22, 24) on needle #3.

Round 1 Needle #1, K until 3 sts remain, K2tog, K 1. On needle #2, K across. On needle #3, K 1, SSK, K to end.

> This first decrease round is a good chance to take care of that extra stitch that you may have picked up along one side of your heel flap. For example, if you have 22 sts on needle #1 and 23 sts on needle #3, do the decrease on needle #1 and omit it on needle #3 for one time only. Thus, you will have an even number of stitches on both sides of your heel flap.

Round 2 Knit.

Repeat Rounds 1 and 2 until you have 9 (10, 12, 13, 15) sts on needle #1, 18 (20 24, 26, 30) on needle #2, and 9 (10, 12, 13, 15) on needle #3.

> You have shaped your heel and returned to the same number of stitches you cast on.

FOOT

Work until piece measures 5½" (6½", 7½", 8½", 9") from the back of the heel to the base of the big toe, approximately 2" shorter than the desired finished size.

TOE

Round 1 Needle #1: work until 3 sts remain, K2tog, K 1. Needle #2: K 1, SSK, K until 3 sts remain, K2tog, K 1. Needle #3: K 1, SSK, K to end.

Round 2 Knit.

Repeat Rounds 1 and 2 until 5 (7, 8, 9, 10) sts remain on needle #1, 10 (14, 16, 18, 20) sts remain on needle #2, and 5 (7, 8, 9, 10) sts remain on needle #3.

Then repeat Round 1 until a total of 8 sts remain (4 sts on 2 needles).

Graft these 8 stitches by using Kitchener stitch. (See page 41)

WORKING WITH SELF-STRIPING YARN

When using a self-striping yarn for an embellishment, it can be helpful to cut the yarn at each color change and make mini-balls of the skein, so that you can better control the placement of color of your embellishments in your work and at the same time have only one color per embellishment.

FINISHING

KNITTED-IN I-CORD DREADS (See opposite page)

Working from the top of the sock down, slip 2 sts from one of the safety pins or stitch holders onto a DPN. Then pick up 1 st from the right-hand "V" on the left side of the CO Sts and 1 st from the from the left-hand "V" on the right side, for a total of 4 sts on the needle. Using CC yarn and leaving a 6" tail, K one row. Slide sts to the other end of the DPN and K across again. Continue knitting a row and sliding the work to the opposite end of the needle, making an I-cord. Knit until the I-cord measures 7". Leaving a 6" tail, cut yarn, thread through sts, and work in the loose end. At the base of the I-cord, thread a tapestry needle, tighten up I-cord, and work in the end into the I-cord itself. Repeat for each stitch holder on the top row.

On the second row of stitch holders, make the I-cords 6½" long.

On the third row of stitch holders, make the I-cords 6" long.

On the fourth row of stitch holders, make the I-cords 5½" long.

On the fifth row of stitch holders, make the I-cords 5" long.

Cut elastic to snugly fit calf at the top of sock, and using sewing thread, stitch ends together. Allow the 10 rounds of reverse st st to roll downward, and insert the elastic into the roll. Hem the roll in place.

Work in all loose ends.

KNITTED-IN I-CORDS

1 For placement of I-cord, slip 2 sts onto small stitch holder.

2 Using a backward loop, cast on 2 sts to replace the ones on the holder.

3 Knit until piece is complete. Then slip the held stitches onto a DPN.

4 Pick up the right-hand "V" of the next stitch.

5 Slide stitches to the opposite end and pick up the left-hand "V" of the stitch to the right.

6 Attach working yarn, leaving a 6" tail long enough to work in when finished. Note: The picked-up stitch may be twisted (as in the photograph) and should be knitted in the back of the stitch. Knit across, then slide the stitches to the opposite end and knit across again, slightly pulling the working yarn in the back. Continue until desired length of the I-cord.

7 Work the end down through the center of the I-cord.

8 Using the original tail, cinch up any loose stitches at the base of the I-cord and work back up through the I-cord.

9 The finished back will be clean, and the I-cord will be neatly knitted in.

For video instructions please visit:
www.youtube.com/watch?v=rE9qNH2AT08

FIESTA

Sometimes simplicity is the best approach. What could be simpler than a bevy of colorful pompoms scattered around the leg of a classic sock? And if you dare, you can add broad stripes of bold colors that encircle the leg. Or take another approach and highlight the leg and foot of one sock using bright colors, and then choose another set of strong colors for the mate. Just think of the fun you can have using all those small tidbits of leftover yarns!

SIZES	CM:6" (CL:7", AS:8", AM:9", AL:10") leg circumference
GAUGE	8 stitches per inch

YARN	Fingering Weight
	For Socks (MC):
	    Color A: 1 Skein (400-425 yds) Cherry Tree Hill, Supersock Solids, Teal Green 100% Merino Wool
	For Pompoms (CC):
	    40-50 yds of stash yarn in bright colors for each pompom
	Waste yarn for provisional cast-on (optional)

NEEDLES	DPN size 1 (2.25 mm), or size to obtain gauge
NOTIONS	Tapestry needle Markers (optional) Pompom maker or circles of heavy cardstock Size C (2.75 mm) crochet hook for provisional cast-on (optional)

LEG

For the edge of this sock you have two options: a knitted-in hem where you use a Provisional Cast-On, or a Turned Edge where you do a regular cast-on and hem when finished.

Provisional Cast-On (See page 105): Using waste yarn, CO 48 (56, 64, 72, 80) sts, distributed onto DPNs as follows:

    Needle #1: 12 (14, 16, 18, 20)
    Needle #2: 24 (28, 32, 36, 40)
    Needle #3: 12 (14, 16, 18, 20)

Join, being careful not to twist.

K 8 rounds, P1 round, K 8 rounds, remove the provisional cast-on, place the stitches on DPNs and then, using a third needle, k2tog, taking 1 st from the front needle and 1 from the back needle. Thus, you will have a neat "finished" hem.

Turned Edge: CO 48 (56, 64, 72, 80) sts, distributed onto DPNs as follows:

    Needle #1: 12 (14, 16, 18, 20)
    Needle #2: 24 (28, 32, 36, 40)
    Needle #3: 12 (14, 16, 18, 20)

Join, being careful not to twist.

Knit 8 rounds. (These rounds will be turned to form a hem during the finishing process.)

Next round: Purl. (This round makes the turning of the hem cleaner and easier.)

Knit until piece measures 5½" (6½", 7½", 8½", 9½"), ending with the last st on needle #2.

A

HEEL FLAP

Beginning on needle #3 (RS), *Sl 1 as if to P, K 1, repeat from *, working across needles 3 and 1. You now have a total of 24 (28, 32, 36, 40) sts on each of the 2 needles. (The stitches held on needle #2 will be worked later for the instep.)

Row 1 Turn work (WS). Sl 1 purlwise, P to end of row.

Row 2 Turn work (RS). *Sl 1 purlwise, K 1, repeat from * across row.

Repeat Rows 1 and 2 for a total of 24 (28, 32, 36, 40) rows, ending with row 1.

TURNING THE HEEL (Short Rows)

Row 1 (RS) K 14 (16, 18, 20, 22), SSK, K 1, turn work.

Row 2 (WS) Sl 1 purlwise, P5, P2tog, P 1, turn work.

Row 3 Sl 1 purlwise, K until 1 st before the gap formed on last row, SSK (bringing together the st before and the st after the gap). K 1. Turn work.

Row 4 Sl 1 purlwise, P until 1 st before the gap formed on last row, P2tog (1 st before the gap and 1 st after the gap), P 1. Turn work.

Repeat rows 3 and 4 until all sts have been worked, ending on row 4 (WS). In some sizes the last 2 rows may not have a single stitch to knit or purl, so end those 2 rows with the decrease of SSK or P2tog. You will have 14 (16, 18, 20, 22) sts remaining.

GUSSET

Working on the heel flap, K 7 (8, 9, 10, 11) sts. With a new needle (which becomes needle #1), K 7 (8, 9, 10, 11) sts. On the same needle, pick up 12-14 (14-16, 16-18, 18-20, 20-22) sts along the side of the heel flap.

Work across needle #2 (the instep stitches that have been waiting patiently). For needle #3, pick up 12-14 (14-16, 16-18, 18-20, 20-22) sts from the other side of the heel flap, and then K the 7 (8, 9, 10, 11) sts from the heel flap. You should now have (more or less) 20 (23, 26, 29, 32) on needle #1, 24 (28, 32, 36, 40) sts on needle #2, and 20 (23, 26, 29, 32) on needle #3.

Round 1 Needle #1: K until 3 sts remain, K2tog, K 1. Needle #2: K across. Needle #3: K 1, SSK, K to end.

> This first decrease round is a good chance to take care of that extra stitch that you may have picked up along one side of your heel flap. For example, if you have 22 sts on needle #1 and 23 sts on needle #3, do the decrease on needle #1 and omit it on needle #3 for one time only. Thus, you will have an even number of stitches on both sides of your heel flap.

Round 2 Knit.

Repeat Rounds 1 and 2 until you have 12 (14, 16, 18, 20) sts on needle #1, 24 (28, 32, 36, 40) on needle #2, and 12 (14, 16, 18, 20) on needle #3.

> You have shaped your heel and returned to the same number of stitches you cast on.

ATTACHING EMBELLISHMENTS

A nice trick when attaching embellishments to a finished sock is to use the yarn color of the main sock rather than the yarn from the embellishment. That way you can knot or sew the embellishment in and work the loose ends into the main body of the sock, to hide these ends more neatly.

FOOT

Knit until piece measures 5½" (6½", 7½", 8½", 9") from the back of the heel to the base of the big toe, approximately 2" shorter than the desired finished size.

TOE

Round 1 Needle #1: work until 3 sts remain, K2tog, K 1. Needle #2: K 1, SSK, K until 3 sts remain, K2tog, K 1. Needle #3: K 1, SSK, K to end.

Round 2 Knit.

Repeat Rounds 1 and 2 until 5 (7, 8, 9, 10) sts remain on needle #1, 10 (14, 16, 18, 20) sts on needle #2, and 5 (7, 8, 9, 10) sts on needle #3.

Then repeat Round 1 until a total of 8 sts remain (4 sts on 2 needles).

Graft these 8 sts by using Kitchener stitch. (See page 41)

FINISHING

Work in all loose ends.

If you chose the Turned Edge option for the sock top, turn at the picot edge and hem carefully.

TO MAKE POMPOMS (See opposite page)

Cut a pair of cardstock circles 1¼" in diameter. Then cut a ½" circle in the center of each circle. Hold the circles together and wrap yarn through the center hole until it is completely full. Cut into the 2 circles at the outer edge. Slightly separate the circles, and using the MC, tie tightly. Make 7-9 pompoms for each sock.

Fluff the pompom and trim. Scatter the pompoms around the leg of the sock, making sure to leave approximately an inch from the heel flap. Securely sew in place.

POMPOMS

Although there are a number of gadgets on the market today that help making a pompom easy, here is an old-fashioned way to make them.

1 Make 2 circles of heavy cardstock, the diameter of finished pompom. Cut a center that is one fourth of the diameter.

2 With a tapestry needle, wrap yarn around both circles, being careful to distribute evenly as you go.

3 Wrap until the center is firmly filled.

4 Carefully cut the yarn at the edge, between the 2 cardboard circles.

5 With yarn that matches the color of the piece to which you will apply the pompom, make a loop and pull the ends through, and then securely tie the pompom.

6 Remove the cardstock circles and trim to shape.

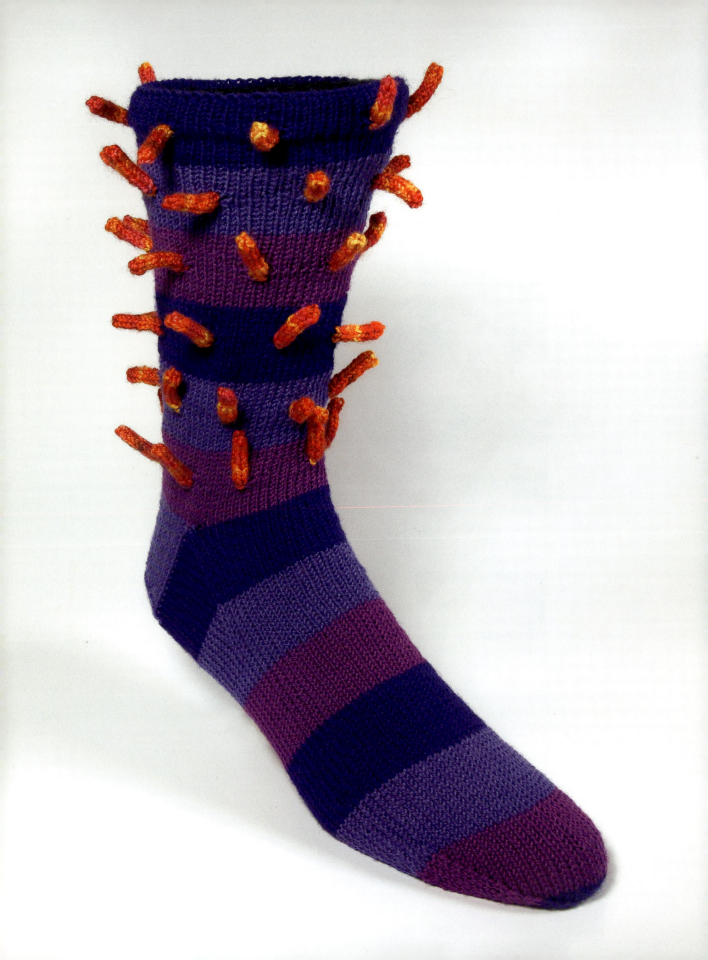

FIRECRACKER

I am not sure why I call this sock Firecracker. Perhaps it was the colors I selected. Regardless, making an overall pattern is always a safe bet, and the color just adds to the success. Variations within this concept can be exciting as well. What would happen if you made the "firecrackers" more random in their placement instead of so evenly spaced? Think about how much fun it would be to play around with the lengths of the I-cords, making some shorter and some longer. How you treat the details will certainly add yet another dimension to these easy and cheerful socks.

SIZES CM: 6" (CL: 7", AS: 8", AM: 9", AL: 10") leg circumference

GAUGE 8 stitches per inch

YARN Fingering Weight
Color A: 100-125 yds Cherry Tree Hill, Supersock Solids, Amethyst 100% Merino Wool
Color B: 100-125 yds Cherry Tree Hill, Supersock Solids, Purple 100% Merino Wool
Color C: 100-125 yds Cherry Tree Hill, Supersock Solids, Mulberry 100% Merino Wool
Color D: 100-125 yds Cherry Tree Hill, Supersock, Brights 100% Merino Wool

NEEDLES DPN size 1 (2.25 mm), or size to obtain gauge

NOTIONS Tapestry needle
Markers (optional)
72 (84, 96, 108, 120) Coilless safety pins or small stitch holders

LEG

Make a turned purl edge, as follows:

Using color A, CO 48 (56, 64, 72, 80) sts, distributed onto DPNs as follows:

Needle #1: 12 (14, 16, 18, 20)
Needle #2: 24 (28, 32, 36, 40)
Needle #3: 12 (14, 16, 18, 20)

Join, being careful not to twist.

Knit 8 rounds. (These rounds will be turned to form a hem during the finishing process.)

Next round: Purl. (This round makes the turning of the hem cleaner and easier.)

Beginning with next round, *K 10 (12, 13, 14, 16) rounds of color A, then 10 (12, 13, 14, 16) rounds of color B, then 10 (12, 13, 14, 16) rounds of color C. Repeat from * for a total of 6 stripes, ending with the last st on needle #2.

> To avoid a horizontal stripe "jog" at each color change, K the first round in the new color, then slip the first st of the second round.

To prepare for knitted-in I-cords, on stripes 1, 3, and 5 on round 5 (6, 6, 7, 8), *sl 2 sts onto a safety pin or holder, using the backward loop method, CO 2 sts, K6, repeat from * around. On stripes 2, 4, and 6, K4, * sl 2 sts onto a holder. Then using the backward loop method, CO 2 sts, K6, repeat from * around. (See page 29)

HEEL FLAP

Using color B and beginning on needle #3 (RS), *Sl 1 as if to P, K 1, repeat from *, working across needles 3 and 1. You now have a total of 24 (28, 32, 36, 40) sts on each of the 2 needles. (The stitches held on needle #2 will be worked later for the instep.)

Row 1 Turn work (WS). Sl 1 purlwise, P to end of row.

Row 2 Turn work (RS). *Sl 1 purlwise, K 1, repeat from * across row.

Repeat Rows 1 and 2 for a total of 24 (28, 32, 36, 40) rows, ending with row 1.

TURNING THE HEEL (Short Rows)

Row 1 (RS) K 14 (16, 18, 20, 22), SSK, K 1, turn work.

Row 2 (WS) Sl 1 purlwise, P 5, P2tog, P 1, turn work.

Row 3 Sl 1 purlwise, K until 1 st before the gap formed on last row, SSK (bringing together the st before and the st after the gap). K 1. Turn work.

Row 4 Sl 1 purlwise, P until 1 st before the gap formed on last row, P2tog (1 st before the gap and 1 st after the gap), P 1. Turn work.

Repeat rows 3 and 4 until all sts have been worked, ending on row 4 (WS). In some sizes the last 2 rows may not have a single stitch to knit or purl, so end those 2 rows with the decrease of SSK or P2tog. You will have 14 (16, 18, 20, 22), sts remaining.

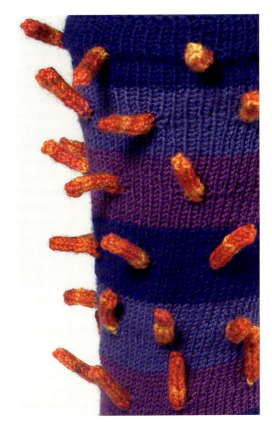

GUSSET

Working on the heel flap, K 7 (8, 9, 10, 11) sts. Change to color A and with a new needle (which becomes needle #1), K 7 (8, 9, 10, 11) sts. On the same needle, pick up 12-14 (14-16, 16-18, 18-20, 20-22) sts along the side of the heel flap.

Work across needle #2 (the instep stitches that have been waiting patiently). For needle #3, pick up 12-14 (14-16, 16-18, 18-20, 20-22) sts from the other side of the heel flap, and then K the 7 (8, 9, 10, 11) sts from the heel flap. You should now have (more or less) 20 (23, 26, 29, 32) on needle #1, 24 (28, 32, 36, 40) sts on needle #2, and 20 (23, 26, 29, 32) on needle #3.

Round 1 Needle #1: K until 3 sts remain, K2tog, K 1. Needle #2: K across. Needle #3: K 1, SSK, K to end.

> This first decrease round is a good chance to take care of that extra stitch that you may have picked up along one side of your heel flap. For example, if you have 22 sts on needle #1 and 23 sts on needle #3, do the decrease on needle #1 and omit it on needle #3 for one time only. Thus, you will have an even number of stitches on both sides of your heel flap.

Round 2 Knit.

Working in established stripes, repeat Rows 1 and 2 until you have 12 (14, 16, 18, 20) sts on needle #1, 24 (28, 32, 36, 40) on needle #2, and 12 (14, 16, 18, 20) on needle #3.

> You have shaped your heel and returned to the same number of stitches you cast on.

COILLESS SAFETY PINS

Safety pins make great stitch holders for small numbers of stitches. Look for special "coilless" safety pins that do not have the circular loop at the end. No chance for your stitches to get caught in a loop if there isn't a loop there!

FOOT

Knit in established stripe pattern, ending after the fifth stripe (color B) counting from the picked-up gusset stitches.

TOE

Change to color B.

Round 1 Needle #1: work until 3 sts remain, K2tog, K 1. Needle #2: K 1, SSK, K until 3 sts remain, K2tog, K 1. Needle #3: K 1, SSK, K to end.

Round 2 Knit.

Maintaining stripe pattern, repeat Rounds 1 and 2 until 5 (7, 8, 9, 10) sts remain on Needle #1, 10 (14, 16, 18, 20) sts on Needle #2, and 5 (7, 8, 9, 10) sts on Needle #3.

Then repeat Round 1 until a total of 8 sts remain (4 sts on 2 needles).

Graft these 8 sts by using Kitchener stitch. (See page 41)

FINISHING

Knitted-in I-cords: Working from the top of the sock down, slip 2 sts from one of the safety pins or stitch holders onto a DPN. Then pick up 1 st from the left-hand "V" on the left side of the CO sts and 1 st from the right-hand "V" on the right side, for a total of 4 sts on the needle. Using color D yarn and leaving a 6" tail, K one row. Slide sts to the other end of the DPN and K across again. Continue knitting a row and sliding the work to the opposite end of the needle, making an I-cord. Knit until the I-cord measures 1¼". Leaving a 6" tail, cut yarn, thread through sts, and work in the loose end. At the base of the I-cord, thread a tapestry needle, tighten up I-cord, and work in the end into the I-cord itself. Repeat for each stitch holder. (See page 29)

Work in all loose ends.

After the I-cords have been attached, turn top edge at the purl round and hem for a neat cuff.

KITCHENER STITCH GRAFTING

The Kitchener stitch does not have to be so daunting . . . There are a couple of things to remember to make working it easier. Remember that each stitch must be worked TWICE . . . either as a knit stitch on one pass and a purl stitch on the second pass . . . or just the opposite.

Working with the same number of stitches on two needles, hold the needles in left hand with wrong side facing the wrong side.

1 Thread a tapestry needle and insert into the first stitch on the front needle as if to PURL . . . leave this stitch on the needle.

2 Thread yarn through the back needle as if to KNIT and leave that stitch on the needle.

3 Thread yarn through stitch on front needle as if to KNIT and SLIP that stitch off . . . then on the same needle, thread through next stitch as if to PURL and LEAVE it on the needle.

4 Thread yarn through the stitch on the back needle as if to PURL and SLIP that stitch off . . . then on the same needle, thread through the next stitch as if to KNIT and LEAVE it on the needle.

5 Repeat #3 and #4 until one stitch remains on each needle. Thread the yarn through the front stitch as if to KNIT and SLIP off the needle, and through the back stitch as if to PURL and SLIP off the needle. Adjust tension to match the tension of the work. Weave in ends.

. . . .

Except for the first pass through the front and back needles (Steps 1 & 2), remember that KNIT stitches are usually the front of the work . . . and therefore when working the two stitches on the front needle, start! with a KNIT stitch . . . the front! Likewise, since the PURL stitch is usually the back side . . . remind yourself when working on the back needle that the purl stich comes first on the back row. Hope that helps!

. . . .

FIREFLY

Since I was a child, fireflies have fascinated me. The twinkle, the sparkle, and the magic they add to the early night sky are so appealing. Somehow, when I see a swarm of fireflies . . . or lightnin' bugs, as we call them in the South . . . I know all is right with the world. Here, the fireflies flutter to life around the ankle of a simple sock with tiny finger cords and simple floss ties on the ends. The whimsy and movement work together to capture that special childhood excitement.

SIZES	CM: 6" (CL: 7", AS: 8", AM: 9", AL: 10") leg circumference
GAUGE	8 stitches per inch
YARN	Fingering Weight
	For Socks:
	Color A: 2 Skeins (400-425 yds) Spud & Chloë, Fine/sock, Color 7800 Popcorn 80% wool, 20% Silk
	For Bobbles:
	Color B: 20 yards Spud & Chloë, Fine/sock, 7811 Bumble Bee 80% wool, 20% Silk
	For I-cords:
	Color C: 20 yards Spud & Chloë, Fine/sock, 7810 Lipstick 80% wool, 20% Silk
	For Finger Cords:
	Color D: 1 Skein (200 yds) Spud & Chloë, Fine/sock, 7804 Cricket 80% wool, 20% Silk
	For Accent:
	Color E: 3-4 yards embroidery floss
	Waste yarn for provisional cast-on
NEEDLES	DPN size 1 (2.25 mm), or size to obtain gauge
NOTIONS	Tapestry needle
	Markers (optional)
	24 (28, 32, 36, 40) Coilless safety pins or small stitch holders
	Small embroidery needle for floss
	Size C (2.75 mm) crochet hook for provisional cast-on (optional)

TO MAKE A BOBBLE (MB) (See page 47)

Working in 1 stitch, KFB twice, then K in the same stitch once more. (1 stitch is now 5 stitches)

Turn work and P 5 sts
Turn work and K 5 sts
Turn work and P 5 sts
Turn work and K 5 sts

Slip left needle into second st on the right needle and pass over (4 sts remain in Bobble). Continue passing sts over from right needle until one st remains.

LEG

For the edge of this sock you have two options: a knitted-in hem where you use a Provisional Cast-On, or a Turned Edge where you do a regular cast-on and hem when finished.

Provisional Cast-On (See page 105): Using waste yarn, CO 48 (56, 64, 72, 80) sts, distributed onto DPNs as follows:

    Needle #1: 12 (14, 16, 18, 20)
    Needle #2: 24 (28, 32, 36, 40)
    Needle #3: 12 (14, 16, 18, 20)

Join, being careful not to twist.

K 8 rounds, work a picot edge (K2tog, YO around), K 8 rounds. Remove the provisional cast-on, place the stitches on DPNs and then, using a third needle, k2tog, taking 1 st from the front needle and 1 from the back needle. Thus, you will have a neat "finished" hem.

Turned Edge: Using color A, CO 48 (56, 64, 72, 80) sts, distributed onto DPNs as follows:

>Needle #1: 12 (14, 16, 18, 20)
>Needle #2: 24 (28, 32, 36, 40)
>Needle #3: 12 (14, 16, 18, 20)

Join, being careful not to twist.

Knit 8 rounds. (These rounds will be turned to form a hem during the finishing process.)

For Picot edge: Next round: *K2tog, YO. Repeat from * across round.

Knit until piece measures 4" (5", 6", 7", 8").

Next round: *Using color B, MB on first st, using color A, K 3, repeat from * across round.

Using color A: K 2 rounds.

Next Round: Prepare for knitted-in I-cords: *K 2, slip 2 sts onto a safety pin, then using backward loop method, CO 2 sts, repeat from * around. (See page 29)

K 2 rounds.

Next round: *Using color B, MB on first st. Using color A, K 3, repeat from * around, bringing the new yarn under at each color change.

Knit until piece measures 5½" (6½", 7½", 8½", 9½"), ending with the last st on needle #2.

HEEL FLAP

Beginning on needle #3 (RS), *Sl 1 as if to P, K 1, repeat from *, working across needles 3 and 1. You now have a total of 24 (28, 32, 36, 40) sts on each of the 2 needles. (The stitches held on needle #2 will be worked later for the instep.)

Row 1 Turn work (WS). Sl 1 purlwise, P to end of row.

Row 2 Turn work (RS). *Sl 1 purlwise, K 1, repeat from * across row.

Repeat Rows 1 and 2 for a total of 24 (28, 32, 36, 40) rows, ending with row 1.

TURNING THE HEEL (Short Rows)

Row 1 (RS) K 14 (16, 18, 20, 22), SSK, K 1, turn work.

Row 2 (WS) Sl 1 purlwise, P 5, P2tog, P 1, turn work.

Row 3 Sl 1 purlwise, K until 1 st before the gap formed on last row, SSK (bringing together the st before and the st after the gap). K 1. Turn work.

Row 4 Sl 1 purlwise, P until 1 st before the gap formed on last row, P2tog (1 st before the gap and 1 st after the gap), P 1. Turn work.

Repeat rows 3 and 4 until all sts have been worked, ending on row 4 (WS). In some sizes the last 2 rows may not have a single stitch to knit or purl, so end those 2 rows with the decrease of SSK or P2tog. You will have 14 (16, 18, 20, 22) sts remaining.

GUSSET

Working on the heel flap, K 7 (8, 9, 10, 11) sts. With a new needle (which becomes needle #1), K 7 (8, 9, 10, 11) sts. On same needle, pick up 12-14 (14-16, 16-18, 18-20, 20-22) sts along the side of the heel flap.

Work across needle #2 (the instep stitches that have been waiting patiently). For needle #3, pick up 12-14 (14-16, 16-18, 18-20, 20-22) sts from the other side of the heel flap, and then K the 7 (8, 9, 10, 11) sts from the heel flap. You should now have (more or less) 20 (23, 26, 29, 32) on needle #1, 24 (28, 32, 36, 40) sts on needle #2, and 20 (23, 26, 29, 32) on needle #3.

Round 1 Needle #1, K until 3 sts remain, K2tog, K 1. On Needle #2 K across. On Needle #3, K 1, SSK, K to end.

This first decrease round is a good chance to take care of that extra stitch that you may have picked up along one side of your heel flap. For example, if you have 22 sts on needle #1 and 23 sts on needle #3, do the decrease on needle #1 and omit it on needle #3 for one time only. Thus, you will have an even number of stitches on both sides of your heel flap.

Round 2 Knit.

Repeat Rounds 1 and 2 until you have 12 (14, 16, 18, 20) sts on needle #1, 24 (28, 32, 36, 40) on needle #2, and 12 (14, 16, 18, 20) on needle #3.

You have shaped your heel and returned to the same number of stitches you cast on.

FOOT

Work until piece measures 5½" (6½", 7½", 8½", 9") from the back of the heel to the base of the big toe, approximately 2" shorter than the desired finished size.

TOE

Round 1 Needle #1: K until 3 sts remain, K2tog, K 1. Needle #2: K 1, SSK, K until 3 sts remain, K2tog, K 1. Needle #3: K 1, SSK, K to end.

Round 2 Knit.

Repeat Rounds 1 and 2 until 5 (7, 8, 9, 10) sts remain on needle #1, 10 (14, 16, 18, 20) sts on needle #2, and 5 (7, 8, 9, 10) sts on needle #3.

Then repeat Round 1 until a total of 8 sts remain (4 sts on 2 needles).

Graft these 8 sts by using Kitchener stitch. (See page 41)

BOBBLES

1 Work to the desired location of bobble. Knit in the front of the stitch as usual. Then K in the back of the same stitch, K in the front of the same stitch again, K in the back of same stitch again, and once more K in the front of the same stitch, for a total of 5 stitches where there was originally 1.

2 Turn the work and P the 5 sts of the bobble.

3 Turn the work and K the 5 sts of the bobble. Then turn and P. Then turn and K.

4 Insert the left needle into the fourth stitch of the bobble and pass that stitch over. Repeat into the third, the second, and the first stitches.

5 You will be left with one stitch, as you began. Gently position the bobble to the front of the work and K the next stitch snugly to tighten and position the bobble into place.

For video instructions please visit:
www.youtube.com/watch?v=3N3yKnTGqQA

FINISHING

KNITTED-IN I-CORD (See page 29)

Working from the top of the sock down, slip 2 sts from one of the safety pins or stitch holders onto a DPN. Then pick up 1 st from the left-hand "V" on the left side of the CO sts and 1 st from the right-hand "V" on the right side, for a total of 4 sts on the needle. Using Color C and leaving a 6" tail, K one row. Slide sts to the other end of the DPN and K across again. Continue knitting a row and sliding the work to the opposite end of the needle, making an I-cord. Knit until the I-cord measures 1½". Leaving a 6" tail, cut yarn, thread through sts, and work in the loose end. At the base of the I-cord, thread a tapestry needle, tighten up I-cord, and work in the end into the I-cord itself. Repeat for each stitch holder. (See page 29)

Using a 30" length of Color D, make 24 (28, 32, 36, 40) finger cords (See page 23) for each sock.

Using a tapestry needle, securely attach each finger cord between the bobbles by pulling the ends to the back and tying a square knot. Work in the ends by pulling them back up into a bobble or looped I-cord.

For accent, thread embroidery floss through the end of each I-cord, tie securely with a square knot, and then clip to about ¼".

If you chose the Turned Edge option for the sock top, turn at the picot edge and hem carefully.

Work in any loose ends.

JESTER

Something about the idea of harlequins and jesters has always intrigued me, so I had to create a Jester Sock. Using 4 colors of yarn in three lengths of dangling triangles adds personality and playfulness to this sock, which is fun and easy to make. Using the three-needle attachment technique makes the inside as smooth and uninterrupted as possible. A nice surprise was the unexpected spiraling effect of each triangle, adding to the whimsy and delight of this special sock. If you are so inclined, you might even add a jingle bell or two.

JESTE

SIZES CM: 6" (CL: 7", AS: 8", AM: 9", AL: 10") leg circumference

GAUGE 8 stitches per inch

YARN Fingering Weight
Color A: 1 Skein (400-425 yds) Berroco, Ultra Alpaca Fine, Color 1285 Oceanic Mix
50% Peruvian Wool, 20% Super Fine Alpaca, 30% Nylon
Color B: 100 yds Berroco, Ultra Alpaca Fine, Color 127 Pea Soup Mix
50% Peruvian Wool, 20% Super Fine Alpaca, 30% Nylon
Color C: 200 yds Berroco, Ultra Alpaca Fine, Color 1281 Redwood
50% Peruvian Wool, 20% Super Fine Alpaca, 30% Nylon
Color D: 200 yds Berroco, Ultra Alpaca Fine, Color 1277 Peat Mix
50% Peruvian Wool, 20% Super Fine Alpaca, 30% Nylon
Waste yarn for provisional cast-on (optional)

NEEDLES Two sets of DPN, size 1 (2.50 mm), or size to obtain gauge
One 24"-36" circular needle, size 1 (2.50 mm), or size to obtain gauge

NOTIONS Tapestry needle,
Markers (optional)
Size C (2.75 mm) crochet hook for provisional cast-on (optional)

TO MAKE A POINT

Make 24 points, as follows:

Using circular needle, make 8 short points, alternating colors A and C

CO 3 sts
Knit 4 rows.
Next row: K 1, KFB, K 1.
Knit 4 rows.
Next row: K2, KFB, K 1
Knit 4 rows.
Next row: K2, KFB, K2
Knit 4 rows.
Next row: K3, KFB, K2
Knit 4 rows.
Next row: K3, KFB, K3
Knit 4 rows.
Cut yarn and leave on the circular needle.

Make 8 medium points, alternating colors B and D. Same as short points, except K 6 rows instead of 4 between the increase rows.

Make 8 long points, alternating colors A and C. Same as short points, except K 8 rows instead of 4 between the increase rows.

LEG

For the edge of this sock you have two options: a knitted-in hem where you use a Provisional Cast-On, or a Turned Edge where you do a regular cast-on and hem when finished.

Provisional Cast-On (See page 105): Using waste yarn, CO 48 (56, 64, 72, 80) sts, distributed onto DPNs as follows:

> Needle #1: 12 (14, 16, 18, 20)
> Needle #2: 24 (28, 32, 36, 40)
> Needle #3: 12 (14, 16, 18, 20)

Join, being careful not to twist.

K 8 rounds, P 1 round, K 8 rounds, remove the provisional cast-on, place the stitches on DPNs and then, using a third needle, k2tog, taking 1 st from the front needle and 1 from the back needle. Thus, you will have a neat "finished" hem.

Turned Edge: Using color A and DPNs, CO 48 (56, 64, 72, 80) sts, distributed onto DPNs as follows:

> Needle #1: 12 (14, 16, 18, 20)
> Needle #2: 24 (28, 32, 36, 40)
> Needle #3: 12 (14, 16, 18, 20)

Join, being careful not to twist.

Knit 8 rounds. (These rounds will be turned to form a hem during the finishing process.)

Next round: Purl. (This round makes the turning of the hem cleaner and easier.)

If you chose the Provisional Cast-On, K 3 (4, 5, 6, 7) rounds.

If you chose the Turned Edge, K 11 (12, 13, 14, 15) rounds.

At this point, the top hem has been determined, and regardless of which cast-on option you chose, continue your work as follows:

Change to color B and K 3 rounds.

At each color change, to avoid a horizontal stripe "jog," K the first round in the new color, then slip the first st of the second round.

Change to color A and K 3 rounds.

Using the three-needle attachment (See page 15) attach short points by holding the circular needle with the knitted short points on top of your work and parallel with needle #1 of your DPN. K2tog by knitting 1 st from the circular needle together with 1 st from the DPN. Do this around, thus attaching 8 short points of alternating colors.

I found it is best to work in the ends of these points as you go. Otherwise it gets very confusing, with lots of dangling ends everywhere. When sewing in the ends of the points where they are attached to the sock, tug slightly to even the tension of the two pieces.

Continuing with color A, K 2 rounds.

K 4 sts of next round and attach medium points, as described above.

Continuing with color A, K 2 rounds.

Attach long points as described above.

Continuing with color A, K 2 rounds.

Change to color B, and K 3 rounds.

Change to color C, and K 11 (12, 13, 14, 15) rounds.

Change to color B, and K 3 rounds.

Change to color D, and K 11 (12, 13, 14, 15) rounds.

Change to color B, and K 3 rounds.

Change to color A, and K 11 (12, 13, 14, 15) rounds.

Change to color B, and K 3 rounds.

Change to color C, and K 5 (6, 6, 7, 7) rounds, ending with the last st on needle #2.

HEEL FLAP

Beginning on needle #3 (RS), change to color D. *Sl 1 as if to P, K 1, repeat from *, working across needles 3 and 1. You now have a total of 24 (28, 32, 36, 40) sts on each of the 2 needles. (The stitches held on needle #2 will be worked later for the instep.)

Row 1 Turn work (WS). Sl 1 purlwise, P to end of row.

Row 2 Turn work (RS). *Sl 1 purlwise, K 1, repeat from * across row.

Repeat Rows 1 and 2 for a total of 24 (28, 32, 36, 40) rows, ending with row 1.

TURNING THE HEEL (Short Rows)

Row 1 (RS) K 14 (16, 18, 20, 22), SSK, K 1, turn work.

Row 2 (WS) Sl 1 purlwise, P 5, P2tog, P 1, turn work.

Row 3 Sl 1 purlwise, K until 1 st before the gap formed on last row, SSK (bringing together the st before and the st after the gap). K 1. Turn work.

Row 4 Sl 1 purlwise, P until 1 st before the gap formed on last row, P2tog (1 st before the gap and 1 st after the gap), P 1. Turn work.

Repeat rows 3 and 4 until all sts have been worked, ending on row 4 (WS). In some sizes the last 2 rows may not have a single stitch to knit or purl, so end those 2 rows with the decrease of SSK or P2tog. You will have 14 (16, 18, 20, 22) sts remaining.

KNITTED-IN HEMS

An easy and tidy way to finish the hem of a turned edge, like a picot edge or a purl edge, is to use a waste yarn and do a provisional cast-on (See page 105). After you work your edge, K 8 rounds, work a picot or purl edge, K 8 rounds, remove the provisional cast-on, placing the stitches on DPNs, and then, using a third needle, K2tog, taking one stitch from the front needle and one from the back needle. Thus, you will have a neat, finished hem, and you can continue with the pattern.

GUSSET

Working on the heel flap, K 7 (8, 9, 10, 11) sts. With a new needle (which becomes needle #1), change to color C and K 7 (8, 9, 10, 11) sts. On the same needle, pick up 12-14 (14-16, 16-18, 18-20, 20-22) sts along the side of the heel flap.

Work across needle #2 (the instep stitches that have been waiting patiently). For needle #3, pick up 12-14 (14-16, 16-18, 18-20, 20-22) sts from the other side of the heel flap, and then K the 7 (8, 9, 10,11) sts from the heel flap. You should now have (more or less) 20 (23, 26, 29, 32) on needle #1, 24 (28, 32, 36, 40) sts on needle #2, and 20 (23, 26, 29, 32) on needle #3. (Note: As you pick up color C, you will be working on round 6 (7, 7, 8, 8) of your stripe.)

Round 1 Needle #1, K until 3 sts remain, K2tog, K 1. On needle #2, K across. On needle #3, K 1, SSK, K to end.

> This first decrease round is a good chance to take care of that extra stitch that you may have picked up along one side of your heel flap. For example, if you have 22 sts on needle #1 and 23 sts on needle #3, do the decrease on needle #1 and omit it on needle #3 for one time only. Thus, you will have an even number of stitches on both sides of your heel flap.

Round 2 Knit.

Maintaining the pattern of colored stripes established in the leg, repeat Rounds 1 and 2 until you have 12 (14, 16, 18, 20) sts on needle #1, 24 (28, 32, 36, 40) on needle #2, and 12 (14, 16, 18, 20) on needle #3.

> You have shaped your heel and returned to the same number of stitches you cast on.

Then K in stripe pattern as established in the leg, changing to 3 rounds of B, then 11 (12, 13, 14, 15) rounds of A, 3 rounds of B, then 11 (12, 13, 14, 15) rounds of C, then 3 rounds of B, etc., ending with 9 (10, 11, 12, 13) rounds in color A. At this point, you will be ready to begin decreasing for the toe.

TOE

Continue working in established stripe pattern, beginning with the last 2 rounds of color B, changing to 3 rounds of B, then D, B, and C, in stripe pattern as established.

Round 1 Needle #1: work until 3 sts remain, K2tog, K 1. Needle #2: K 1, SSK, K until 3 sts remain, K2tog, K 1. Needle #3: K 1, SSK, K to end.

Round 2 Knit.

Repeat Rounds 1 and 2 until 5 (7, 8, 9, 10) sts remain on needle #1, 10 (14, 16, 18, 20) sts on needle #2, and 5 (7, 8, 9, 10) sts on needle #3.

Then repeat Round 1 until a total of 8 sts remain (4 sts on 2 needles).

Graft these 8 sts by using Kitchener stitch. (See page 41)

FINISHING

Work in all loose ends.

If you chose the Turned Edge option for the sock top, turn at the picot edge and hem carefully.

JULIE'S SOCK

One afternoon my friend Julie wore a striking sweater to our local yarn shop. Simple in its design, the sweater featured bold horizontal striping and a vividly colored ruffle running along the front edges, the bottom and around the neck. The boldness of the black and white in contrast with the bright ruffle inspired me to make a sock. Julie was thrilled, and I hope you will be too . . . a sock that is so easy to make and easy to change with playful color. Experiment with different colors for the stripes and the trim and don't forget to have fun!

JULIE

SIZES	CM:6" (CL:7", AS:8", AM:9", AL:10") leg circumference
GAUGE	8 stitches per inch
YARN	Fingering Weight
	Color A: 50 yards Cascade, Heritage, #5632
	75% Superwash Merino Wool / 25% Nylon
	Color B: 50 yards Cascade, Heritage, #5633
	75% Superwash Merino Wool / 25% Nylon
	Color C: 1 Skein (400-425 yds) Cascade, Heritage, #5601
	75% Superwash Merino Wool / 25% Nylon
	Color D: 1 Skein (400-425 yds) Cascade, Heritage, #5618
	75% Superwash Merino Wool / 25% Nylon
NEEDLES	Two set of DPN size 1 (2.25 mm), or size to obtain gauge
	One 16" size 1 (2.25 mm) circular, or size to obtain gauge
NOTIONS	Tapestry needle
	Markers (optional)

LEG

Using circular needle and Color A, CO 192 (224, 256, 288, 320) sts.

Join, being careful not to twist. Place marker to designate beginning of round.

Purl 3 rounds.

Change to color B and K 2 rounds.

> To avoid a horizontal stripe "jog," here and at all following color changes, K the first round in the new color, then slip the first st of the second round.

K2tog around.

Beginning with a purl round, work in garter stitch (alternating knit and purl rounds) for a total of 7 rounds.

Change to DPNs and K2tog around, distributing sts onto DPNs as follows:

> Needle #1: 12 (14, 16, 18, 20)
> Needle #2: 24 (28, 32, 36, 40)
> Needle #3: 12 (14, 16, 18, 20)

Knit 10 rounds.

Change to color C.

Knit 11 (13, 15, 17, 19) rounds.

Change to color D.

Knit 11 (13, 15, 17, 19) rounds.

Change to color C, K 11 (13, 15, 17, 19) rounds.

Change to color D, K 11 (13, 15, 17, 19) rounds.

Change to color C, K 11 (13, 15, 17, 19) rounds, ending on needle #2.

HEEL FLAP

Change to color A. Beginning on needle #3 (RS),*Sl 1 as if to P, K 1, repeat from *, working across needles 3 and 1. You now have a total of 24 (28, 32, 36, 40) sts on each of the 2 needles. (The stitches held on needle #2 will be worked later for the instep.)

Row 1 Turn work (WS). Sl 1 purlwise, P to end of row.

Row 2 Turn work (RS). *Sl 1 purlwise, K 1, repeat from * across row.

Repeat Rows 1 and 2 for a total of 24 (28, 32, 36, 40) rows, ending with row 1.

TURNING THE HEEL (Short Rows)

Row 1 (RS) K 14 (16, 18, 20, 22), SSK, K 1, turn work.

Row 2 (WS) Sl 1 purlwise, P5, P2tog, P 1, turn work.

Row 3 Sl 1 purlwise, K until 1 st before the gap formed on last row, SSK (bringing together the st before and the st after the gap). K 1. Turn work.

Row 4 Sl 1 purlwise, P until 1 st before the gap formed on last row, P2tog (1 st before the gap and 1 st after the gap), P 1. Turn work.

Repeat rows 3 and 4 until all sts have been worked, ending on row 4 (WS). In some sizes the last 2 rows may not have a single stitch to knit or purl, so end those 2 rows with the decrease of SSK or P2tog. You will have 14 (16, 18, 20, 22) sts remaining.

GUSSET

Working on the heel flap, K 7 (8, 9, 10, 11) sts. With a new needle (which becomes needle #1), K 7 (8, 9, 10, 1) sts. On the same needle and changing to color D, pick up 12-14 (14-16, 16-18, 18-20, 20-22) sts along the side of the heel flap.

Work across needle #2 (the instep stitches that have been waiting patiently). For needle #3, pick up 12-14 (14-16, 16-18, 18-20, 20-22) sts from the other side of the heel flap, and then K the 7 (8, 9, 10, 11) sts from the heel flap. You should now have (more or less) 20 (23, 26, 29, 32) on needle #1, 24 (28, 32, 36, 40) sts on needle #2, and 20 (23, 26, 29, 32) on needle #3.

Round 1 Needle #1: K until 3 sts remain, K2tog, K 1. Needle #2: K across. Needle #3: K 1, SSK, K to end.

This first decrease round is a good chance to take care of that extra stitch that you may have picked up along one side of your heel flap. For example, if you have 22 sts on needle #1 and 23 sts on needle #3, do the decrease on needle #1 and omit it on needle #3 for one time only. Thus, you will have an even number of stitches on both sides of your heel flap.

Round 2 Knit.

Maintaining the stripe pattern established in the leg, repeat Rounds 1 and 2 until you have 12 (14, 16, 18, 20) sts on needle #1, 24 (28, 32, 36, 40) on needle #2, and 12 (14, 16, 18, 20) on needle #3.

You have shaped your heel and returned to the same number of stitches you cast on.

JOGLESS STRIPING

There are a number of different techniques and approaches to creating a "jogless" stripe, so that the stripes align when working in the round and changing from one color to another. For my money, the easiest and most effective is to simply slip the first stitch of the second round of the new color. Your jog will almost disappear!

FOOT

Knit in the stripe pattern established in the leg for a total of 5 stripes from the heel, approximately 2" shorter than the desired finished size.

TOE

Change to color A:

Round 1 Needle #1: work until 3 sts remain, K2tog, K 1. Needle #2: K 1, SSK, K until 3 sts remain, K2tog, K 1. Needle #3: K 1, SSK, K to end.

Round 2 Knit.

Repeat Rounds 1 and 2 until 5 (7, 8, 9, 10) sts remain on needle #1, 10 (14, 16, 18, 20) sts on needle #2, and 5 (7, 8, 9, 10) sts on needle #3.

Then repeat Round 1 until a total of 8 sts remain (4 sts on 2 needles).

Graft these 8 sts by using Kitchener stitch. (See page 41)

FINISHING

Work in all loose ends.

HEEL FLAPS

It isn't absolutely necessary to always count the rows of the heel flap. Just remember that the heel flap is approximately a square, so an easy way to make sure it is long enough is to simply fold your work over diagonally. If the row with slipped stitches at the top of the needle aligns with the first row of the heel flap, you are probably where you need to be.

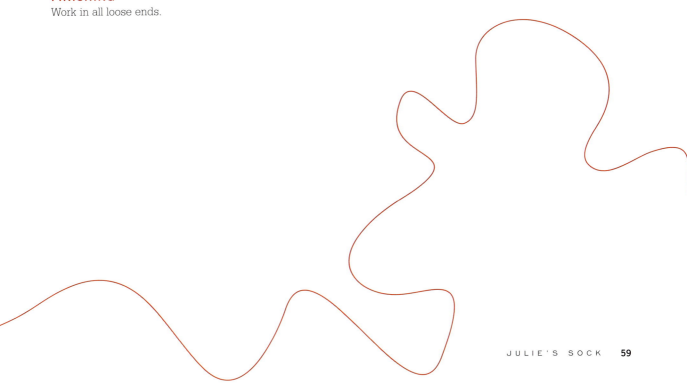

LOOOOOOOOOPS

This simple sock carries a lot of punch. It is certainly easy to make an I-cord. And with only a little knitting experience, it is easy to make a simple sock. Combine the two, and you have a sock that is magical and playful. The sock pictured has the loops going around the top. Think how much fun they would be going around the ankle too. As pictured, the I-cord is 14 feet . . . yes, 14 feet! . . . long. Make it 25 feet and see what happens. Don't let the idea of making such long I-cords turn you off. Luckily, small gadgets are available that will crank out beautiful I-cords as fast as you can turn the handle. What a great way to turn a simple sock into a super sock!

SIZES	CM: 6" (CL: 7", AS: 8", AM: 9", AL: 10") leg circumference
GAUGE	8 stitches per inch
YARN	Fingering Weight
	For socks: (MC):
	3 Skeins (400-425 yds) Soxx Appeal, Color #9765
	96% Superwash Merino Wool, 3% nylon, 1% elastic
	For I-cord loops (CC):
	1 Skein (400-425 yds) Ty-Dy Socks, Color #1672
	80% Superwash Wool, 20% nylon
	Waste yarn for provisional cast-on (optional)
NEEDLES	DPN size 1 (2.50 mm), or size to obtain gauge
NOTIONS	Tapestry needle
	Markers (optional)
	Size C (2.75 mm) crochet hook for provisional cast-on (optional)

LEG

For the edge of this sock you have two options: a knitted-in hem where you use a Provisional Cast-On, or a Turned Edge where you do a regular cast-on and hem when finished.

Provisional Cast-On (See page 105): Using waste yarn, CO 48 (56, 64, 72, 80) sts, distributed onto DPNs as follows:

    Needle #1: 12 (14, 16, 18, 20)
    Needle #2: 24 (28, 32, 36, 40)
    Needle #3: 12 (14, 16, 18, 20)

Join, being careful not to twist.

K 8 rounds, P 1 round, K 8 rounds, remove the provisional cast-on, place the stitches on DPNs and then, using a third needle, k2tog, taking 1 st from the front needle and 1 from the back needle. Thus, you will have a neat "finished" hem.

Turned Edge: Using MC, CO 48 (56, 64, 72, 80) sts, distributed onto DPNs as follows:

    Needle #1: 12 (14, 16, 18, 20)
    Needle #2: 24 (28, 32, 36, 40)
    Needle #3: 12 (14, 16, 18, 20)

Join, being careful not to twist.

Knit 8 rounds. (These rounds will be turned to form a hem during the finishing process.)

Next round: Purl. (This round makes the turning of the hem cleaner and easier.)

Using either cast-on method, knit until piece measures 5½" (6½", 7½", 8½", 9½") from the purl round, ending with the last st on needle #2.

HEEL FLAP

Beginning on needle #3 (RS), *Sl 1 as if to P, K 1, repeat from * working across needles 3 and 1. You now have a total of 24 (28, 32, 36, 40) sts on each of the 2 needles. (The stitches held on needle #2 will be worked later for the instep.)

Row 1 Turn work (WS). Sl 1 purlwise, P to end of row.

Row 2 Turn work (RS). *Sl 1 purlwise, K 1, repeat from * across row.

Repeat Rows 1 and 2 for a total of 24 (28, 32, 36, 40) rows, ending with row 1.

TURNING THE HEEL (Short Rows)

Row 1 (RS) K 14 (16, 18, 20, 22), SSK, K 1, turn work.

Row 2 (WS) Sl 1 purlwise, P 5, P2tog, P 1, turn work.

Row 3 Sl 1 purlwise, K until 1 st before the gap formed on last row, SSK (bringing together the st before and the st after the gap). K 1. Turn work.

Row 4 Sl 1 purlwise, P until 1 st before the gap formed on last row, P2tog (1 st before the gap and 1 st after the gap), P 1. Turn work.

Repeat rows 3 and 4 until all sts have been worked, ending on row 4 (WS). In some sizes the last 2 rows may not have a single stitch to knit or purl, so end those 2 rows with the decrease of SSK or P2tog. You will have 14 (16, 18, 20, 22) sts remaining.

GUSSET

Working on the heel flap, K 7 (8, 9, 10, 11) sts. With a new needle (which becomes needle #1), K 7 (8, 9, 10, 11) sts. On the same needle, pick up 12-14 (14-16, 16-18, 18-20, 20-22) sts along the side of the heel flap.

Work across needle #2 (the instep stitches that have been waiting patiently). For needle #3, pick up 12-14 (14-16, 16-18, 18-20, 20-22) sts from the other side of the heel flap, and then K the 7 (8, 9, 10, 11) sts from the heel flap. You should now have (more or less) 20 (23, 26, 29, 32) on needle #1, 24 (28, 32, 36, 40) sts on needle #2, and 20 (23, 26, 29, 32) on needle #3.

Round 1 Needle #1: K until 3 sts remain, K2tog, K 1. Needle #2: K across. Needle #3: K 1, SSK, K to end.

> This first decrease round is a good chance to take care of that extra stitch that you may have picked up along one side of your heel flap. For example, if you have 22 sts on needle #1 and 23 sts on needle #3, do the decrease on needle #1 and omit it on needle #3 for one time only. Thus, you will have an even number of stitches on both sides of your heel flap.

Round 2 Knit.

Repeat Rounds 1 and 2 until you have 12 (14, 16, 18, 20) sts on needle #1, 24 (28, 32, 36, 40) on needle #2, and 12 (14, 16, 18, 20) on needle #3.

> You have shaped your heel and returned to the same number of stitches you cast on.

FOOT

Work until piece measures 5½" (6½", 7½", 8½", 9") from the back of the heel to the base of the big toe, approximately 2" shorter than the desired finished size.

TOE

Round 1 Needle #1: work until 3 sts remain, K2tog, K 1. Needle #2: K 1, SSK, K until 3 sts remain, K2tog, K 1. Needle #3: K 1, SSK, K to end.

Round 2 Knit.

Repeat Rounds 1 and 2 until 5 (7, 8, 9, 10) sts remain on needle #1, 10 (14, 16, 18, 20) sts on needle #2, and 5 (7, 8, 9, 10) sts on needle #3.

Then repeat Round 1 until a total of 8 sts remain (4 sts on 2 needles).

Graft these 8 sts by using Kitchener stitch. (See page 41)

I-CORDS MADE EASY

Making an I-cord as an embellishment is easy and effective. If you have a lot of I-cord to make, you might invest in a small machine that produces I-cord as fast as you can turn a crank. Most of these machines, available at most craft stores, can only accommodate a DK or fingering weight yarn. Try it . . . you might like it!

FINISHING
Work in all loose ends.

MAKE I-CORD
Using DPNs, Using CC, CO 5 sts. Knit 1 round. Do not turn but slide sts to opposite end of DPN and K across the round. Repeat these 2 rounds until the I-cord measures at least 14 feet. Cut yarn and pull through the stitches. Using tapestry needle, sew one end of the I-cord to the other (closing the loop), and work in loose ends.

TO ATTACH I-CORD
Pin both ends of the I-cord to the top purl edge of the sock and securely attach, using the MC. (Using the MC to sew in the I-cord will make the inside of the sock look cleaner, as no contrasting yarn will show.) If you used the crocheted provisional cast-on, attach the I-cords just below the hemmed edge. To attach, run tapestry needle through the I-cord for about ¼", and then pull the two ends to the back and secure tightly with a square knot. (Only a small amount of space is available for each loop to attach it, so to make sure that it is secure the knot seems to be the best answer. I know you are never supposed to put a knot in a knitted garment, but in this case it seems called for.) Leave tails about 6" long so they can be more easily worked in. Arrange the I-cord around the top of the sock in varying lengths of loops, holding in place with a safety pin or basting yarn until you can permanently attach.

If you chose the Turned Edge option for the sock top, turn at the picot edge and hem carefully.

PEBBLES

The inspiration for this sock came one fall afternoon when I looked across a friend's patio and saw how the unraked leaves had amassed along the edge of the lawn and then scattered. I used bobbles to interpret the leaf idea, and when I finished the sock the name "Pebbles" seemed more appropriate. It would be fun to play with the coloring of these pebbles, varying rows of different-colored pebbles, scattering colors across the sock. Here I used a heather-colored yarn for the main sock and a self-striping one for the bobbles. Regardless of how you choose to arrange your colors, this sock demonstrates how you can always rely on Mother Nature for inspiration.

SIZES	CM: 6" (CL: 7", AS: 8", AM: 9", AL: 10") leg circumference
GAUGE	8 stitches per inch

YARN	Fingering Weight
	For Socks (MC):
	    2 Skeins (400-425 yds) Blue Moon Fiber Arts, Silkie Socks That Rock, Color Brick
	    81% Superwash Merino, 19% Silk
	For Bobbles (CC):
	    1 Skein (300 yds) Blue Moon Fiber Arts, Silkie Socks That Rock, Color Farmhouse
	    81% Superwash Merino, 19% Silk

NEEDLES	Two sets of DPN size 1 (2.25 mm), or size to obtain gauge
NOTIONS	Tapestry needle Markers (optional)

TO MAKE A BOBBLE (MB) (See page 47)

Working in a single stitch, KFB twice, then K in the same stitch once more. (One stitch is now 5 stitches)

Turn work and P 5 sts
Turn work and K 5 sts
Turn work and P 5 sts
Turn work and K 5 sts

Slip the left needle into the second st on the right needle and pass it over. (4 sts remain in the bobble). Continue passing sts over from right needle until one st remains.

LEG

CO 48 (56, 66, 72, 78) sts, as follows:

Needle #1: 12 (14, 17, 18, 19)
Needle #2: 24 (28, 32, 36, 40)
Needle #3: 12 (14, 17, 18, 19)

To accommodate the repeat of the bobble chart, the number of sts for AS has been increased by 2 sts and for AL decreased by 2 sts. These changes will be corrected on the beginning row of the heel flap.

Join, being careful not to twist.

Knit 8 rounds. (These rounds will be turned to form a hem during the finishing process.)

On the next round, begin working the bobble chart, starting with round 4 (1, 1, 1, 1) and ending with round 42 (55, 67, 67, 67). Work the bobbles in CC and the main body of the sock in MC.

> For a neater finished look, between bobbles, "strand" CC yarn by carrying for 3 sts and then bringing the CC underneath the MC.

Knit until piece measures 5½" (6½", 7½", 8½", 9½"), ending with the last st on needle #2.

HEEL FLAP

Beginning on needle #3 (RS), *Sl 1 as if to P, K 1, repeat from *, working across needles 3 and 1. (Note: For size AS, K2tog in first 2 sts on needle #3 and K2tog the last 2 sts on needle #1. For size AL, M1 in the first st on needle #3 and M1 on the last st of needle #1. This increase or decrease adjusts the stitch count that was changed to accommodate the repeat of the bobble chart.) You now have a total of 24 (28, 32, 36, 40) sts on each of the 2 needles. (The stitches held on needle #2 will be worked later for the instep.)

Row 1 Turn work (WS). Sl 1 purlwise, P to end of row.

Row 2 Turn work (RS). *Sl 1 purlwise, K 1, repeat from * across row.

Repeat Rows 1 and 2 for a total of 24 (28, 32, 36, 40) rows, ending with row 1.

TURNING THE HEEL (Short Rows)

Row 1 (RS) K 14 (16, 18, 20, 22), SSK, K 1, turn work.

Row 2 (WS) Sl 1 purlwise, P5, P2tog, P 1, turn work.

Row 3 Sl 1 purlwise, K until 1 st before the gap formed on last row, SSK (bringing together the st before and the st after the gap). K 1. Turn work.

Row 4 Sl 1 purlwise, P until 1 st before the gap formed on last row, P2tog (1 st before the gap and 1 st after the gap), P 1. Turn work.

Repeat rows 3 and 4 until all stitches have been worked, ending on row 4 (WS). In some sizes the last 2 rows may not have a single stitch to knit or purl, so end those 2 rows with the decrease of SSK or P2tog. You will have 14 (16, 18, 20, 22) sts remaining.

GUSSET

Working on the heel flap, K 7 (8, 9, 10, 11) sts. With a new needle (which becomes needle #1), K 7 (8, 9, 10, 11) sts. On the same needle, pick up 12-14 (14-16, 16-18, 18-20, 20-22) sts along the side of the heel flap.

Work across needle #2 (the instep stitches that have been waiting patiently). For needle #3, pick up 12-14 (14-16, 16-18, 18-20, 20-22) sts from the other side of the heel flap, and then K the 7 (8, 9, 10, 11) sts from the heel flap. You should now have (more or less) 20 (23, 26, 29, 32) sts on needle #1, 24 (28, 32, 36, 40) sts on needle #2, and 20 (23, 26, 29, 32) on needle #3.

Round 1 Needle #1: K until 3 sts remain, K2tog, K 1. Needle #2: K across. Needle #3: K 1, SSK, K to end.

> This first decrease round is a good chance to take care of that extra stitch that you may have picked up along one side of your heel flap. For example, if you have 23 sts on needle #1 and 22 sts on needle #3, do the decrease on needle #1 and omit it on needle #3 for one round only. Then you will have an equal number of stitches on both sides of your heel flap.

Round 2 Knit.

Repeat Rounds 1 and 2 until you have 12 (14, 16, 18, 20) sts on needle #1, 24 (28, 32, 36, 40) on needle #2, and 12 (14, 16, 18, 20) on needle #3.

> You have shaped your heel and returned to the same number of stitches you cast on.

FOOT

Knit until piece measures 5½" (6½", 7½", 8½", 9") from the back of the heel to the base of the big toe, approximately 2" shorter than the desired finished size.

TOE

Round 1 Needle #1: work until 3 sts remain, K2tog, K 1. Needle #2: K 1, SSK, K until 3 sts remain, K2tog, K 1. Needle #3: K 1, SSK, K to end.

Round 2 Knit.

Repeat Rounds 1 and 2 until 5 (7, 8, 9, 10) sts remain on needle #1, 10 (14, 16, 18, 20) sts on needle #2, and 5 (7, 8, 9, 10) sts on needle #3.

Then repeat Round 1 until a total of 8 sts remain (4 sts on 2 needles).

Graft these 8 sts by using Kitchener stitch. (See page 41)

FINISHING

Work in all loose ends.

At the first row of bobbles, turn the first 8 rounds inward and hem to form a neat cuff.

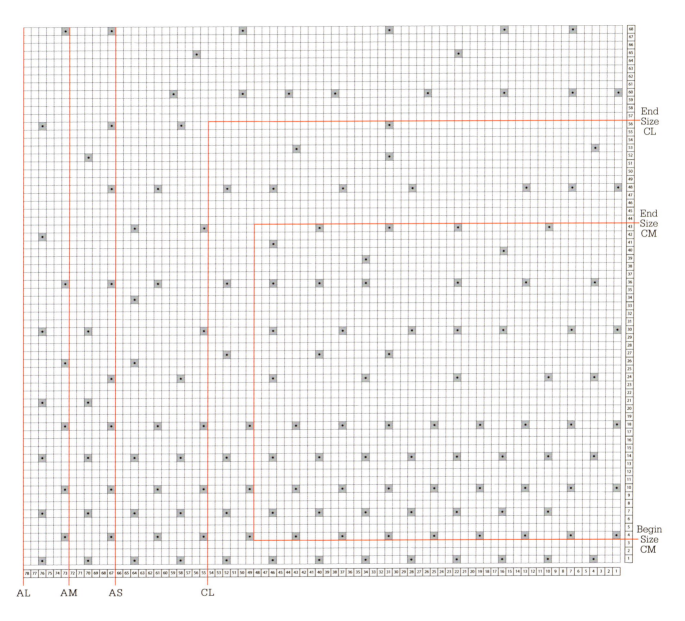

RIPPLES

As I work on a project until I am relaxed and can enjoy the process of just knitting, my mind begins to wander and think about what I am going to make next. I think, "What if?" For this sock, I thought "what if I picked up the ladder between rows of stitches? What could I do with such a ladder?" I made a small sample and in doing so I got the idea of ruffles running up the leg of the sock. It worked! Using a solid yarn for the basic sock allowed the self-striping yarn for the ruffles to stand out. In changing the expected repeat of the self-striping yarn from the diameter of the foot to the long ruffles running the length of the sock leg, the stripes became solids and further enhanced their effectiveness. As a second benefit, simply picking up the ladders made the inside of the sock as finished as the outside. Your fellow knitters will look at this sock and ask "How did you do that?" It's easy. Ripple away!

SIZES CM:6" (CL:7", AS:8", AM:9", AL:10") leg circumference

GAUGE 8 stitches per inch

YARN Fingering Weight
For socks: (MC):
  1 Skein (400-425 yds) Berroco, Ultra Alpaca Fine, #1275 Pea Soup Mix
  50% Peruvian Wool, 20% Super Fine Alpaca, 30% Nylon
For Ruffles: (CC):
  1 Skein (200 yds) Ty-Dy Socks, Color 1574
  80% Superwash Wool, 20% Nylon
Waste yarn for provisional cast-on (optional)

NEEDLES Two sets of DPN size 1 (2.25 mm), or size to obtain gauge
One 16" size 1 (2.25 mm) circular, or size to obtain gauge

NOTIONS Tapestry needle
Markers (optional)

LEG

For a turned purl edge:

Using MC, CO 48 (56, 64, 72, 80) sts, distributed onto DPNs, as follows:

   Needle #1: 12 (14, 16, 18, 20)
   Needle #2: 24 (28, 32, 36, 40)
   Needle #3: 12 (14, 16, 18, 20)

Join, being careful not to twist.

Knit 8 rounds. (These rounds will be turned to form a hem during the finishing process.)

Next round: Purl. (This round makes the turning of the hem cleaner and easier.)

Knit until piece measures 5½" (6½", 7½", 8½", 9½") from the purl round, ending with the last st on needle #2.

HEEL FLAP

Beginning on needle #3 (RS), *Sl 1 as if to P, K 1, repeat from *, working across needles 3 and 1. You now have a total of 24 (28, 32, 36, 40) sts on each of the 2 needles. (The stitches held on needle #2 will be worked later for the instep.)

Row 1 Turn work (WS). Sl 1 purlwise, P to end of row.

Row 2 Turn work (RS). *Sl 1 purlwise, K 1, repeat from * across row.

Repeat Rows 1 and 2 for a total of 24 (28, 32, 36, 40) rows, ending with row 1.

PICKING UP STITCHES IN THE LADDER

1 Using a circular needle or long DPN, insert your needle between two columns of knit stitches to expose the "ladder." Pick up every other "rung" of this ladder until you have the desired number of stitches.

2 Slide the needle to the opposite end and add the working yarn, leaving about a 6" tail. Work in desired pattern, noting any stitches that may be twisted (as shown in the photo).

3 Once worked, the reverse side is clean and neat.

For video instructions please visit:
www.youtube.com/watch?v=mT8DdVOJbug&feature

TURNING THE HEEL (Short Rows)

Row 1 (RS) K 14 (16, 18, 20, 22), SSK, K 1, turn work.

Row 2 (WS) Sl 1 purlwise, P5, P2tog, P 1, turn work.

Row 3 Sl 1 purlwise, K until 1 st before the gap formed on last row, SSK (bringing together the st before and the st after the gap). K 1. Turn work.

Row 4 Sl 1 purlwise, P until 1 st before the gap formed on last row, P2tog (1 st before the gap and 1 st after the gap), P 1. Turn work.

Repeat rows 3 and 4 until all sts have been worked, ending on row 4 (WS). In some sizes the last 2 rows may not have a single stitch to knit or purl, so end those 2 rows with the decrease of SSK or P2tog. You will have 14 (16, 18, 20, 22) sts remaining.

GUSSET

Working on the heel flap, K 7 (8, 9, 10, 11) sts. With a new needle (which becomes needle #1), K 7 (8, 9, 10, 11) sts. On the same needle, pick up 12-14 (14-16, 16-18, 18-20, 20-22) sts along the side of the heel flap.

Work across needle #2 (the instep stitches that have been waiting patiently). For needle #3, pick up 12-14 (14-16, 16-18, 18-20, 20-22) sts from the other side of the heel flap, and then K the 7 (8, 9, 10, 11) sts from the heel flap. You should now have (more or less) 20 (23, 26, 29, 32) on needle #1, 24 (28, 32, 36, 40) sts on needle #2, and 20 (23, 26, 29, 32) on needle #3.

Round 1 Needle #1: K until 3 sts remain, K2tog, K 1. Needle #2: K across. Needle #3: K 1, SSK, K to end.

> This first decrease round is a good chance to take care of that extra stitch that you may have picked up along one side of your heel flap. For example, if you have 22 sts on needle #1 and 23 sts on needle #3, do the decrease on needle #1 and omit it on needle #3 for one time only. Thus, you will have an even number of stitches on both sides of your heel flap.

Round 2 Knit.

Repeat Rounds 1 and 2 until you have 12 (14, 16, 18, 20) sts on needle #1, 24 (28, 32, 36, 40) on needle #2, and 12 (14, 16, 18, 20) on needle #3.

> You have shaped your heel and returned to the same number of stitches you cast on.

FOOT

Work until piece measures 5½" (6½", 7½", 8½", 9") from the back of the heel to the base of the big toe, approximately 2" shorter than the desired finished size.

TOE

Round 1 Needle #1: Work until 3 sts remain, K2tog, K 1. Needle #2: K 1, SSK, K until 3 sts remain, K2tog, K 1. Needle #3: K 1, SSK, K to end.

Round 2 Knit.

Repeat Rounds 1 and 2 until 5 (7, 8, 9, 10) sts remain on needle #1, 10 (14, 16, 18, 20) sts on needle #2, and 5 (7, 8, 9, 10) sts on needle #3.

Then repeat Round 1 until a total of 8 sts remain (4 sts on 2 needles).

Graft these 8 sts by using Kitchener stitch. (See page 41)

TO MAKE RUFFLES

Beginning at the center back just below the purl edge, use the circular needle to pick up every other "rung" or bar in the ladder between the stitches, running straight down the leg and ending 1" above the heel flap. (See page 75)

Using CC color, K 2 rows.

Next row: KFB in each st across row, doubling the number of sts you picked up.

Knit 2 rows.

Next row: KFB in each st across row, once again doubling the number of sts.

Knit 2 rows.

BO loosely.

Begin the next ruffle 6 (7, 8, 9, 10) sts over, for a total of 8 ruffles around the leg.

With tapestry needle, attach the bound-off edge to the base of the picked-up edge to "round off" each end of each ruffle.

FINISHING

Work in all loose ends.

Turn the top edge at the purl row and hem for a neat cuff.

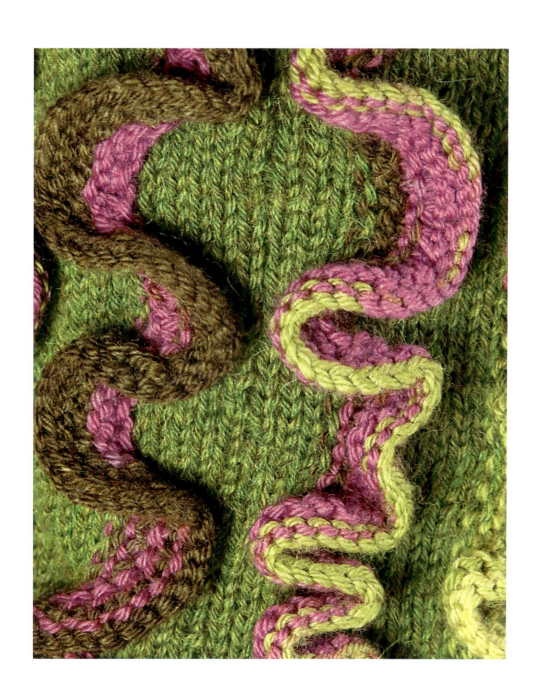

SNAKE IN THE GRASS

"How do you ever think of these crazy socks?" I hear that question all the time. In this case, the name came first. As I pondered the possibilities for entries in Knitter's Magazine and XRX Inc.'s "Think Outside the Sox" contest, I tried to think outside the norm. I made a list of types of socks: standard socks, tabi (or flip-flop) socks, socks for everyday wear, and socks as art. I thought of phases or sayings that could act as a springboard for creative solutions: for example, Snake in the Grass. Once I saw Southwest Trading Company's Tofutsie, I knew it would be the perfect yarn for my Snake. With such a three-dimension concept, the sock had to be a tabi sock. I could just see the beady-eyed snake resting its playful head on the thongs of a flip-flop and wrapping its tail up and around the leg. But what about the "grass?" I remembered a special cording my mother taught me to make years ago. She called it an "idiot's knot." I am not sure where she learned this technique or why she called it an idiot's knot. Mother's cord, a tighter and more dense cording than the I-cord, uses only your fingers and no needles. I've decided to change Momma's name "Idiot's knot" to "finger cord." Four hundred . . . count 'em . . . four hundred finger cords later, I had a winner! My funny flip-flop sock won in SWTC's "creativity" category. I trust my mother would approve.

SIZES	CM: 6" (CL: 7", AS: 8", AM: 9", AL: 10") leg circumference
GAUGE	8 stitches per inch
YARN	Fingering Weight
	For socks, snake, and grass:
	3 Skeins (1200 yds) SWTC, Inc., Tofutsies #854 Four Leaf TOEever
	For Flowers:
	10-15 yds each: SWTC, Inc., Tofutsies #726, #803, #860, and #863
	Waste yarn for provisional cast-on (optional)
NEEDLES	For socks:
	DPN Size 1 (2.50 mm), or size to obtain gauge
	For Snake and Flowers:
	DP Size 4 (3.5 mm)
NOTIONS	Tapestry needle
	Markers (optional)
	Two small red beads for "eyes"
	Polyfoam fiber fill
	Size C (2.75 mm) crochet hook for provisional cast-on (optional)

LEG

For the edge of this sock you have two options: a knitted-in hem where you use a *Provisional Cast-On*, or a *Turned Edge* where you do a regular cast-on and hem when finished.

Provisional Cast-On (See page 105): Using waste yarn, CO 48 (56, 64, 72, 80) sts, distributed onto DPNs as follows:

    Needle #1: 12 (14, 16, 18, 20)
    Needle #2: 24 (28, 32, 36, 40)
    Needle #3: 12 (14, 16, 18, 20)

Join, being careful not to twist.

K 8 rounds, work a picot edge (K2tog, YO around), K 8 rounds, remove the waste yarn, place the stitches on DPNs and then, using a third needle, k2tog, taking 1 st from the front needle and 1 st from the back needle. Thus, you will have a neat "finished" hem.

Turned Edge: Using MC, CO 48 (56, 64, 72, 80) sts, distributed onto DPNs as follows:

    Needle #1: 12 (14, 16, 18, 20)
    Needle #2: 24 (28, 32, 36, 40)
    Needle #3: 12 (14, 16, 18, 20)

Join, being careful not to twist.

Knit 8 rounds.

For picot edge: *K2tog, YO. Repeat from * across round.

Knit until piece measures 5½" (6½", 7½", 8½", 9½"), ending with the last st on Needle #2.

HEEL FLAP

Beginning on Needle #3 (RS): *Sl 1 as if to P, K 1, repeat from * working across needles 3 and 1. You now have a total of 24 (28, 32, 36, 40) sts on each of the 2 needles. (The stitches held on Needle #2 will be worked later for the instep.)

Row 1 Turn work (WS). Sl 1 purlwise, P to end of row.

Row 2 Turn work (RS). *Sl 1 purlwise, K 1, repeat from * across row.

Repeat Rows 1 and 2 for a total of 24 (28, 32, 36, 40) rows, ending with row 1.

TURNING THE HEEL (Short Rows)

Row 1 (RS) K 14 (16, 18, 20, 22), SSK, K 1, turn work.

Row 2 (WS) Sl 1, as if to purl, P 5, P2tog, P 1, turn work.

Row 3 Sl 1 purlwise, K until 1 st before the gap formed on last row, SSK (bringing together the st before and the st after the gap). K 1. Turn work.

Row 4 Sl 1 purlwise, P until 1 st before the gap formed on last row, P2tog (1 st before the gap and 1 st after the gap), P 1. Turn work.

Repeat rows 3 and 4 until all sts have been worked, ending on row 4 (WS). In some sizes the last 2 rows may not have a single stitch to knit or purl, so end those 2 rows with the decrease of SSK or P2tog. You will have 14 (16, 18, 20, 22) sts remaining.

GUSSET

Working on the heel flap, K 7 (8, 9, 10, 11) sts. With a new needle (which becomes needle #1), K 7 (8, 9, 10, 11) sts. On same needle, pick up 12-14 (14-16, 16-18, 18-20, 20-22) sts along the side of the heel flap.

Work across Needle #2 (the instep stitches that have been waiting patiently). For Needle #3, pick up 12-14 (14-16, 16-18, 18-20, 20-22) sts from the other side of the heel flap and then K the 7 (8, 9, 10, 11) sts from the heel flap. You should now have (more or less) 20 (23, 26, 29, 32) on Needle #1, 24 (28, 32, 36, 40) sts on Needle #2, and 20 (23, 26, 29, 32) on Needle #3.

Round 1 Needle #1: K until 3 sts remain, K2tog, K 1. Needle #2: K across. Needle #3: K 1, SSK, K to end.

> This first decrease round is a good chance to take care of that extra stitch that you may have picked up along one side of your heel flap. For example, if you have 22 sts on needle #1 and 23 sts on needle #3, do the decrease on needle #1 and omit it on needle #3 for one time only. Thus, you will have an even number of stitches on both sides of your heel flap.

Round 2 Knit.

Repeat Rounds 1 and 2 until you have 12 (14, 16, 18, 20) sts on needle #1, 24 (28, 32, 36, 40) on needle #2, and 12 (14, 16, 18, 20) on needle #3.

> You have shaped your heel and returned to the same number of stitches you cast on.

FOOT

Work until piece measures 5½" (6½", 7½", 8½", 9") from the back of the heel to the base of the big toe, approximately 2" shorter than the desired finished size.

TABI TOE

LEFT SOCK

On needle #1: Knit 4 (5, 6, 7, 8). For the big toe, slip the next 8 (9, 10, 11, 12) sts from needle #1 and 8 (9, 10, 11, 10) sts from needle #2 onto a holder. Using backward loop method, CO 4 (4, 6, 6, 6) sts to bridge the gap on needle #1. Join to work in the round, being careful not to twist. Continue on needle #2, K until 3 sts remain, K2tog, K 1. On needle #3, K 1, SSK, K to end.

Round 1 Knit.

Round 2 Needle #1: K 8 (9, 12, 13, 14). Needle #2: K until 3 sts remain, K2tog, K 1. Needle #3: K 1, SSK, K to end.

Repeat Rounds 1-2, decreasing at end of needle #2 and at the beginning of needle #3 until 6 (7, 8, 9, 10) sts remain on needle #3.

Then continue the decreases EVERY round until 2 (2, 3, 3, 2) sts remain on needle #3 and 6 (7, 9, 10, 12) on needle #2. Continuing using Needle #3, K 6 (7, 9, 10, 12) sts from Needle #1. Slip remaining 2 (2, 3, 3, 2) sts from needle #1 onto needle #2. Thus, you will have 8 (9, 12, 13, 14) sts on 2 needles. Use Kitchener stitch (See page 41) to graft these stitches together.

FOR BIG TOE

Pick up and K 4 (4, 6, 6, 6) sts from the cast-on bridge and 16 (18, 20, 22, 22) sts from the holder, placing 6 (8, 8, 10, 10) on needle #1 and 7 (7, 9, 9, 9) sts each on needles #2 and 3.

Knit until big toe measures 1½" (or length of toe)

K2tog around [10 (11, 13, 14, 14) sts remain].

Knit 1 round.

K2tog around until last st [5 (6, 7, 7, 7) sts remain].

Cut yarn and pull through the remaining stitches. Draw tight and secure yarn. Work in all ends.

RIGHT SOCK

Knit 12 (14, 16, 18, 20) sts from needle #1 and K 16 (19, 22, 26, 30) from needle #2. Slip remaining 8 (9, 10, 10, 10) sts from needle #2 and first 8 (9, 10, 12, 12) sts from needle #3 onto a holder for big toe.

K remaining 4 (5, 6, 6, 10) sts. Using backward loop method, CO 4 (4, 6, 6, 6) sts on needle #3 to bridge gap.

Round 1 On needle #1, K to last 3 sts, K2tog, K 1. On needle #2, K 1, SSK, K to end. On needle #3, K all sts.

Round 2 Knit

Repeat Rounds 1-2, decreasing at end of needle #1 and beginning of needle #2 until 6 (7, 8, 9, 10) sts remain on needle #1.

Then continue the decreases EVERY round until 2 (2, 3, 3, 2) sts remain on needle #1 and 6 (7, 9, 11, 12) on needle #2. Continue, using Needle #3, K 8 (7, 9, 12, 14). Slip 2 (2, 3, 1, 2) sts from needle #1 onto needle #2. Thus, you will have 8 (9, 12, 13, 14) sts on 2 needles. Use Kitchener stitch to graft these stitches together.

FOR BIG TOE

Pick up and K 4 (4, 6, 6, 6) sts from the cast-on bridge and 16 (18, 20, 22, 22) sts from the holder, placing 6 (8, 8, 10, 10) on needle #1 and 7 (7, 9, 9, 9) sts each on needles #2 and 3.

Knit until big toe measures 1½" (or length of toe)

K2tog around [10 (11, 13, 14, 14) sts remain].

Knit 1 round.

K2tog around until last st [5, 6, 7, 7, 7) sts remain].

Cut yarn and pull through the remaining stitches. Draw tight and secure yarn. Work in all ends.

ALTERNATIVE STANDARD TOE

Round 1 Needle #1: work until 3 sts remain, K2tog, K 1. Needle #2: K 1, SSK, K until 3 sts remain, K2tog, K 1. Needle #3: K 1, SSK, K to end.

Round 2 Knit.

Repeat Rounds 1 and 2 until 5 (7, 8, 9, 10) sts remain on Needle #1, 10 (14, 16, 18, 20) sts on Needle #2, and 5 (7, 8, 9, 10) sts on Needle #3.

Then repeat Round 1 until a total of 8 sts remain (4 sts on 2 needles).

Graft these 8 sts by using Kitchener stitch. (See page 41)

SNAKE

Make one . . . since it is "A" snake in the grass, only one sock gets the snake.

Using two strands of yarn A, CO 3 sts on size 4 DPNs.

Knit one row, slide work to opposite end of needle, and continue to knit, making an I-cord.

Continue making I-cord for 1½", then KFB, for 4 sts on needle.

Using polyfoam, stuff as you go, firmly but not stiffly.

Continue to K until piece measures 4½". KFB (5 sts on needle).

Continue to K until piece measures 7½". KFB (6 sts on needle).

Continue to K until piece measures 12". KFB (7 sts on needle).

Divide 7 sts onto 3 needles: 2 on needle #1, 2 on needle #2, and 3 on needle #3.

At 14", increase to 8 sts.

At 16½", increase to 9 sts.

At 20", increase to 10 sts.

At 22", increase to 11 sts.

At 24", increase to 12 sts.

At 25", place marker (PM), K 1, KFB, K 2, KFB, K 2, KFB, K 2, KFB, K 1.

SHAPING THE SNAKE'S HEAD

Round 1 K 1, KFB, K 4, KFB, K 2, KFB, K 4, KFB, K 1.

Round 2 K 1, KFB, K 6, KFB, K 2, KFB, K 6, KFB, K 1 (24 sts).

Rounds 3, 4, 5 Knit.

Round 6 K 5, K2tog, K 10, K2tog, K 5.

Round 7 Knit.

Round 8 K 4, K2tog, K 9, K2tog, K 5.

Round 9 K 4, K2tog, K 8, K2tog, K 4.

Round 10 K 3, K2tog, K 7, K2tog, K 4.

Round 11 K 3, K2tog, K 6, K2tog, K 3.

Round 12 K 2, K2tog, K 5, K2tog, K 3.

Round 13 K 2, K2tog, K 4, K2tog. K 2.

Round 14 K 1, K2tog, K 3, K2tog, K 2.

Round 15 K 1, K2tog, K 2, K2tog, K 2.

With tapestry needle, run yarn through the remaining 6 sts and tighten, working the end inside.

FINISHING SNAKE

Sew on two small red beads for eyes.

Make a tongue by using single 24" yarn of a contrasting color. See instructions for finger cord under GRASS. Sew tongue in place, pulling excess yarn inside.

Try on the finished sock and place the head of the snake so that it will fall at the base of the big toe. Then wrap the snake around the leg, ending with the tail encircling the top of the sock just under the picot edge. Using contrasting waste yarn, lightly baste the snake in place. Working from the wrong side of the sock and using the same yarn as the snake, securely sew the snake in place, leaving the head free to "flop" over the strap of a flip-flop.

FINISHING TOP EDGE

If you chose the Turned Edge option for the sock top, turn at the picot edge and hem carefully.

GRASS

Finger Cord (See page 23)

Using a 60" length of Color A. Fold in half for a working length of 30". Make approximately 200 individual "blades" of grass for each sock.

First, sew the "snake" onto one sock before you add the "grass."

To attach the grass to the sock, use a tapestry needle and separately pull each thread of the cord through to the back of the sock, going around a stitch or stitch and a half. Tightly knot these ends and work into the back of the sock. Work in these ends.

> When attaching, make sure that you do NOT place any grass on the sole of the sock foot. Likewise, leave the area blank where the flip-flop strap will fall. You may find it helpful to try the sock on with a flip-flop and then, with a contrasting color, lightly baste in a "guideline" where the straps fall.

FLOWERS

Make 14-18 (7-9 for each sock).

Using several colors and doubling the yarn, CO 40, 50, or 60 sts for a variety of sizes.

Working in st st, work 2 or 3 rows, ending with a purl row. Change to a different-colored yarn and K2tog across row. Purl back. Change color and repeat, decrease the row, and purl back. Continue these 2 rows until 4-6 sts remain. With tapestry needle, pull yarn through stitches and tighten. Then seam up the edge of the "flower."

For centers, using a contrasting color, CO 5, K in ST st for 5-6 rows. Pull yarn through stitches and tighten up. Gather up along both edges and the CO row, tighten into a "ball," and sew into the center of the flower.

Scatter finished flowers around socks. I found it fun to strategically place one flower on the big toe of the sock that did not get the snake.

TILE SOCK

What is more beautiful than a traditional tiled roof . . . one tile cascading over another? With so many irresistible multicolored yarns on the market today, what could be a better use for them than this three-dimensional embellishment of tiles cascading down the leg of this sock? Who says you must use these rectangular shapes? Experiment with leaf shapes or shapes with rounded ends or even triangles. Whatever shape you choose, it can be easily attached with the simple three-needle attachment technique (very similar to a three-needle bind-off). Enjoy!

SIZES	CM: 6" (CL: 7", AS: 8", AM: 9", AL: 10") leg circumference
GAUGE	8 stitches per inch

YARN	Fingering Weight
	For Socks (MC):
	    1 Skein (325 yds) Kertzer, On Your Toes Bamboo, Color KOB.2058 Mystical Grape
	    75% Bamboo, 25% Nylon
	For Tiles (CC):
	    1 Skein (400-425 yds) Noro, Kureyon Sock Yarn, Color S188
	    70% Wool, 30% Nylon
	Waste yarn for provisional cast-on (optional)

NEEDLES	Two sets of DPN size 1 (2.25 mm), or size to obtain gauge One 16" size 1 (2.50 mm) circular
NOTIONS	Tapestry needle Markers (optional) Size C (2.75 mm) crochet hook for provisional cast-on (optional)

TO MAKE TILES

Make 48 tiles for each sock.

In order to be able to strategically place the colors of the tile, snip the Noro into small balls as each new color begins. Then as you knit the tiles, think about scattering the colors in a way that appeals to you. If you don't cut the yarn into balls of individual colors, your tiles may be variegated, which is fine too. Your sock . . . your choice.

Using one small ball of CC and circular needle, cast on 6 (7, 8, 9, 10) sts and work in garter stitch for 20 (22, 24, 26, 30) rows. Break yarn, leaving a 6" tail, and leave the tile on the circular needle. Make seven more tiles, being conscious of color placement. You will have a total of 8 tiles "holding" on the circular needle.

LEG

For the edge of this sock you have two options: a knitted-in hem where you use a Provisional Cast-On, or a Turned Edge where you do a regular cast-on and hem when finished.

Provisional Cast-On (See page 105): Using waste yarn, CO 48 (56, 64, 72, 80) sts, distributed onto DPNs as follows:

    Needle #1: 12 (14, 16, 18, 20)
    Needle #2: 24 (28, 32, 36, 40)
    Needle #3: 12 (14, 16, 18, 20)

Join, being careful not to twist.

K 8 rounds, P 1 round.

K 8 rounds, remove the provisional cast-on, place the stitches on DPNs and then, using a third needle, k2tog, taking 1 st from the front needle and 1 st from the back needle. Thus, you will have a neat "finished" hem.

Next round: Place the circular needle in front of the DPN making sure that a purl ridge is facing the knit face of the main sock and *K one st from the circular needle together with one st from the DPN. Repeat from * across the tile, thus attaching the tile to the leg of the sock. Continue around sock.

Knit the next 6 (8, 10, 12, 14) rounds.

Turned Edge: Using main color, CO 48 (56, 64, 72, 80) sts, distributed onto DPNs as follows:

>Needle #1: 12 (14, 16, 18, 20)
>Needle #2: 24 (28, 32, 36, 40)
>Needle #3: 12 (14, 16, 18, 20)

Join, being careful not to twist.

Knit 8 rounds. (These rounds will be turned to form a hem during the finishing process.)

Next round: Purl. (This round makes the turning of the hem cleaner and easier.)

Next round: Place the circular needle in front of the DPN, making sure that a purl ridge is facing the knit face of the main sock.and *K one st from the circular needle together with one st from the DPN. Repeat from * across the tile, thus attaching the tile to the leg of the sock. Continue around sock.

Knit the next 6 (8, 10, 12, 14) rounds.

> After 4-5 rounds, I suggest that you stop and work in the loose ends of the tiles. Doing so will help save you the drudgery and confusion that result from waiting until the last to deal with these ends. Working the ends into the CO edge is straightforward. As for the opposite end of the tile, gently but snugly, tug on the ends where the tiles are attached to even the tension of the sock fabric and the tile fabric.

Using the circular needle, make 8 more tiles, being conscious of the color placement.

Attach the second round of tiles as you did for the original round, starting at the fourth st of the round, so that second round of tiles is staggered from the first.

Knit the next 6 (8, 10, 12, 14) rounds.

Using the circular needle, make 8 more tiles, being conscious of the color placement.

Attach the third round of tiles, beginning on the first st of the round.

Continue to alternate stockinette rounds and tile attachment rounds (remembering to begin with the offset 4 sts on every other attachment round) until you have a total of 6 rounds of tiles.

Knit until piece measures 5½" (6½", 7½", 8½", 9½"), ending with the last st on needle #2.

HEEL FLAP

Beginning on needle #3 (RS), *Sl 1 as if to P, K 1, repeat from *, working across needles 3 and 1. You now have a total of 24 (28, 32, 36, 40) sts on each of the 2 needles. (The stitches held on needle #2 will be worked later for the instep.)

Row 1 Turn work (WS). Sl 1 purlwise, P to end of row.

Row 2 Turn work (RS). *Sl 1 purlwise, K 1, repeat from * across row.

Repeat Rows 1 and 2 for a total of 24 (28, 32, 36, 40) rows, ending with row 1.

TURNING THE HEEL (Short Rows)

Row 1 (RS) K 14 (16, 18, 20, 22), SSK, K 1, turn work.

Row 2 (WS) Sl 1 purlwise, P5, P2tog, P 1, turn work.

Row 3 Sl 1 purlwise, K until 1 st before the gap formed on last row, SSK (bringing together the st before and the st after the gap). K 1. Turn work.

Row 4 Sl 1 purlwise, P until 1 st before the gap formed on last row, P2tog (1 st before the gap and 1 st after the gap), P 1. Turn work.

Repeat rows 3 and 4 until all sts have been worked, ending on row 4 (WS). In some sizes the last 2 rows may not have a single stitch to knit or purl, so end those 2 rows with the decrease of SSK or P2tog. You will have 14 (16, 18, 20, 22) sts remaining.

GUSSET

Working on the heel flap, K 7 (8, 9, 10, 11) sts. With a new needle (which will now be needle #1), K 7 (8, 9, 10, 11) sts. On the same needle, pick up 12-14 (14-16, 16-18, 18-20, 20-22) sts along the side of the heel flap.

Work across needle #2 (the instep stitches that have been waiting patiently). For needle #3, pick up 12-14 (14-16, 16-18, 18-20, 20-22) sts from the other side of the heel flap, and then K the 7 (8, 9, 10, 11) sts from the heel flap. You should now have (more or less) 20 (23, 26, 29, 32) on needle #1, 24 (28, 32, 36, 40) sts on needle #2, and 20 (23, 26, 29, 32) on needle #3.

Round 1 Needle #1: K until 3 sts remain, K2tog, K 1. Needle #2: K across. Needle #3: K 1, SSK, K to end.

> This first decrease round is a good chance to take care of that extra stitch that you may have picked up along one side of your heel flap. For example, if you have 22 sts on needle #1 and 23 sts on needle #3, do the decrease on needle #1 and omit it on needle #3 for one time only. Thus, you will have an even number of stitches on both sides of your heel flap.

Round 2 Knit.

Repeat Rounds 1 and 2 until you have 12 (14, 16, 18, 20) sts on needle #1, 24 (28, 32, 36, 40) on needle #2, and 12 (14, 16, 18, 20) on needle #3.

> You have shaped your heel and returned to the same number of stitches you cast on.

FOOT

Work until piece measures 5½" (6½", 7½", 8½", 9") from the back of the heel to the base of the big toe, approximately 2" shorter than the desired finished size.

TOE

Round 1 Needle #1: work until 3 sts remain, K2tog, K 1. Needle #2: K 1, SSK, K until 3 sts remain, K2tog, K 1. Needle #3: K 1, SSK, K to end.

Round 2 Knit.

Repeat Rounds 1 and 2 until 5 (7, 8, 9, 10) sts remain on needle #1, 10 (14, 16, 18, 20) sts on needle #2, and 5 (7, 8, 9, 10) sts on needle #3.

Then repeat Round 1 until a total of 8 sts remain (4 sts on 2 needles).

Graft these 8 sts by using Kitchener stitch. (See page 41)

FINISHING

If you chose the Turned Edge option for the sock top, at turn at the picot edge and hem carefully.

Work in any loose ends.

TIPTOE THRU THE TULIPS

The inspiration for this sock came very early in the Think Outside the Sox contest, but for various reasons it didn't make the cut and had to wait for this book to make an appearance. The whimsy of a tabi toe, coupled with the idea of traipsing through a field of beautiful tulips, just couldn't be squelched, so here it is! There is nothing difficult about making this sock . . . it just takes a bit of time and patience, and it requires a bit more yarn than usual. (A full skein of yarn is used for each sock for the tulips alone.) Dyeing the tulips with Kool-Aid is a perfect way to capture the feathering of red and yellow found in nature. Although a standard toe is also included, I plan on wearing my flip-flops as I tiptoe thru my tulips!

SIZES CM:6" (CL:7", AS:8", AM:9", AL:10") leg circumference

GAUGE 8 stitches per inch

YARN Fingering Weight
For Socks:
  Color A: 1 Skein (250 yds) Spud & Chloe, Fine Sock, #7806, 80% Wool, 20% Silk, Blue
  Color B: 1 Skein (250 yds) Spud & Chloe, Fine Sock, #7803, 80% Wool, 20% Silk, Brown
For Tulips and Stamen:
  Color C: 2 Skeins (500 yds) Spud & Chloe, Fine Sock, #7800, 80% Wool, 20% Silk, White
For Leaves and Grass:
  Color D: 1 Skein (250 yds) Spud & Chloe, Fine Sock, #7804, 80% Wool, 20% Silk, Green
For accent:
  Black embroidery floss

NEEDLES DPN size 1 (2.25 mm), or size to obtain gauge

NOTIONS Tapestry needle
Markers (optional)
2 pkgs Kool-Aid (no sugar) Cherry
2 pkgs Kool-Aid (no sugar) Lemon
White vinegar
Small brush and/or medicine dropper
Microwave
Microwaveable dish
Elastic for band at top

LEG

Using Color A: (Blue)

CO 48 (56, 64, 72, 80) sts, distributed onto DPNs as follows:

Needle #1: 12 (14, 16, 18, 20)
Needle #2: 24 (28, 32, 36, 40)
Needle #3: 12 (14, 16, 18, 20)

Knit 8 rounds. (These rounds will be turned to form a hem during the finishing process.)

Next round: Purl. (This round makes the turning of the hem cleaner and easier.)

Knit until piece measures 5" (6", 7", 8", 9"). Change to Color B (Brown) and work in Reverse St St for ½", ending with the last st on needle #2.

HEEL FLAP

Continuing with Color B (Brown) and beginning on needle #3 (RS), *Sl 1 as if to P, K 1, repeat from *, working across needles 3 and 1. You now have a total of 24 (28, 32, 36, 40) sts on each of the 2 needles. (The stitches held on needle #2 will be worked later for the instep.)

Row 1 Turn work (WS). Sl 1 purlwise, P to end of row.

Row 2 Turn work (RS). *Sl 1 purlwise, K 1, repeat from * across row.

Repeat Rows 1 and 2 for a total of 24 (28, 32, 36, 40) rows, ending with row 1.

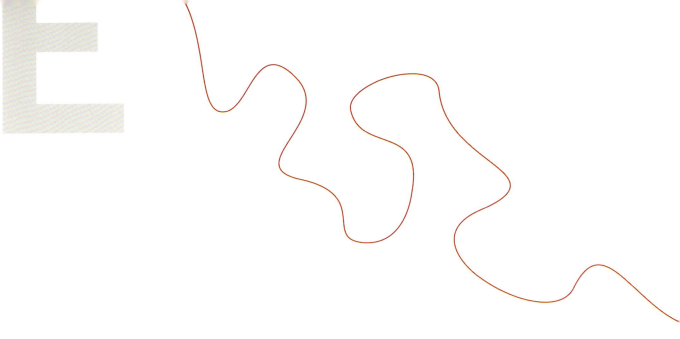

TURNING THE HEEL (Short Rows)

Row 1 (RS) K 14 (16, 18, 20, 22), SSK, K 1, turn work.

Row 2 (WS) Sl 1 purlwise, P 5, P2tog, P 1, turn work.

Row 3 Sl 1 purlwise, K until 1 st before the gap formed on last row, SSK (bringing together the st before and the st after the gap). K 1. Turn work.

Row 4 Sl 1 purlwise, P until 1 st before the gap formed on last row, P2tog (1 st before the gap and 1 st after the gap), P 1. Turn work.

Repeat rows 3 and 4 until all sts have been worked, ending on row 4 (WS). In some sizes the last 2 rows may not have a single stitch to knit or purl, so end those 2 rows with the decrease of SSK or P2tog. You will have 14 (16, 18, 20, 22) sts remaining.

GUSSET

Working on the heel flap, K 7 (8, 9, 10, 11) sts. With a new needle (which becomes needle #1), K 7 (8, 9, 10, 11) sts. On the same needle, pick up 12-14 (14-16, 16-18, 18-20, 20-22) sts along the side of the heel flap.

Work across Needle #2 (the instep stitches that have been waiting patiently). For needle #3, pick up 12-14 (14-16, 16-18, 18-20, 20-22) sts from the other side of the heel flap, and then K the 7 (8, 9, 10, 11) sts from the heel flap. You should now have (more or less) 20 (23, 26, 29, 32) on needle #1, 24 (28, 32, 36, 40) sts on needle #2, and 20 (23, 26, 29, 32) on needle #3.

Row 1 Needle #1: K until 3 sts remain, K2tog, K 1. Needle #2: K across. Needle #3: K 1, SSK, K to end.

This first decrease round is a good chance to take care of that extra stitch that you may have picked up along one side of your heel flap. For example, if you have 22 sts on needle #1 and 23 sts on needle #3, do the decrease on needle #1 and omit it on needle #3 for one time only. Thus, you will have an even number of stitches on both sides of your heel flap.

Row 2 Knit.

Repeat Rows 1 and 2 until you have 12 (14, 16, 18, 20) sts on needle #1, 24 (28, 32, 36, 40) on needle #2, and 12 (14, 16, 18, 20) on needle #3.

You have shaped your heel and returned to the same number of stitches you cast on.

FOOT

Knit until piece measures 5½" (6½", 7½", 8½", 9") from the back of the heel to the base of the big toe, approximately 2" shorter than the finished size.

TABI TOE

LEFT SOCK

Needle #1: Knit 4 (5, 6, 7, 8). For the big toe, slip the next 8 (9, 10, 11, 12) sts from needle #1 and 8 (9, 10, 11, 10) from needle #2 on holder. Using backward loop cast-on, CO 4 (4, 6, 6, 6) sts to bridge the gap on needle #1. Joining to work in the round, being careful not to twist, continue on needle #2, K until 3 sts remain, K2tog, K 1. On needle #3, K 1, SSK, K to end.

Round 1 Knit.

Round 2 Needle #1: K 8 (9, 12, 13, 14). Needle #2: K until 3 sts remain, K2tog, K 1. Needle #3: K 1, SSK, K to end.

Repeat Rounds 1-2, decreasing at end of needle #2 and at the beginning of needle #3 until 6 (7, 8, 9, 10) sts remain on needle #3.

Then continue decrease EVERY round until 2 (2, 3, 3, 2) sts remain on needle #3 and 6 (7, 9, 10, 12) on needle #2. Continuing using Needle #3, K 6 (7, 9, 10, 12) sts from Needle #1. Slip remaining 2 (2, 3, 3, 2) sts on needle #1 onto needle #2. Thus, 8 (9, 12, 13, 14) sts on 2 needles. Using Kitchener stitch (See page 41), graft these stitches together.

FOR BIG TOE

Pick up and K 4 (4, 6, 6, 6) sts from cast-on bridge and 16 (18, 20, 22, 22) sts from holder, placing 6 (8, 8, 10, 10) on needle #1 and 7 (7, 9, 9, 9) sts each on needles #2 and 3.

Knit until big toe measures 1½" (or length of toe.)

K2 tog across round [10 (11, 13, 14, 14) sts remain.]

Knit 1 round.

K2tog across round until last st [5 (6, 7, 7, 7) sts remain.]

Cut yarn and pull through the remaining stitches. Draw tight and secure yarn. Work in all ends.

RIGHT SOCK

Knit 12 (14, 16, 18, 20) sts from Needle #1, K 16 (19, 22, 26, 30) from needle #2, slip remaining 8 (9, 10, 10, 10) sts from needle #2 and first 8 (9, 10, 12, 12) sts from needle #3 onto holder for big toe.

K remaining 4 (5, 6, 6, 10) sts. Using backward loop cast-on, CO 4 (4, 6, 6, 6) sts onto needle #3 to bridge gap.

Round 1 Needle #1: K to last 3 sts, K2tog, K 1. Needle #2: K 1, SSK, K to end. Needle #3: K all sts.

Round 2 Knit.

Repeat Rounds 1-2, decreasing at end of needle #1 and beginning of needle #2 until 6 (7, 8, 9, 10) sts remain on needle #1.

Then continue decreasing EVERY round until 2 (2, 3, 3, 2) sts remain on needle #1 and 6 (7, 9, 11, 12) on needle #2. Continuing using Needle #3, K 8 (7, 9, 12, 14). Slip 2 (2, 3, 1, 2) sts from needle #1 onto needle #2. Thus, you will have 8 (9, 12, 13, 14) sts on 2 needles. Using Kitchener stitch (See page 41), graft these stitches together.

FOR BIG TOE

Pick up and K 4 (4, 6, 6, 6) sts from the cast-on bridge and 16 (18, 20, 22, 22) sts from holder, placing 6 (8, 8, 10, 10) on needle #1 and 7 (7, 9, 9, 9) sts each on needles #2 and 3.

Knit until big toe measures 1½" (or length of toe).

K2 tog across round [10 (11, 13, 14, 14) sts remain.]

Knit 1 round.

K2tog across round until last st [5, 6, 7, 7, 7) sts remain.]

Cut yarn and pull through the remaining stitches. Draw tight and secure yarn. Work in all ends.

ALTERNATE STANDARD TOE

Round 1 Needle #1: work until 3 sts remain, K2tog, K 1. Needle #2: K 1, SSK, K until 3 sts remain, K2tog, K 1. Needle #3: K 1, SSK, K to end.

Round 2 Knit.

Repeat Rounds 1 and 2 until 5 (7, 8, 9, 10) sts remain on needle #1, 10 (14, 16, 18, 20) sts on needle #2, and 5 (7, 8, 9, 10) sts on Needle #3.

Then repeat Round 1 until a total of 8 sts remain (4 sts on 2 needles).

Graft these 8 sts by using Kitchener stitch. (See page 41)

GUSSET PICKED-UP STITCHES

Ideally, you would pick up 1 more stitch than the slipped selvage. This extra stitch helps to prevent that unsightly hole that can appear in your gusset. My experience is that these ideal numbers never seem to work out just right . . . the knitting demons get in the way! So I think it is best to let your work tell you how many stitches to pick up. Don't force stitches, but don't leave gaps. Do your best to pick up the same number of stitches on each side of the heel flap. If, however, you find you have a stitch more or less on one side than the other, don't fret. That can be fixed in the first or second round of your gusset decreases. A difference of 2 or more stitches, however, is too many and should be taken out and reworked.

TULIP PETALS (Make 15 for each sock)

Using Color C, CO 7

Row 1 Purl.

Row 2 KFB in first st, K until 1 st remains, KFB.

Repeat rows 1 and 2 until 19 sts, ending with a purl row.

St St for 8 rows, ending with a purl row.

Row 1 K2tog on first st, K until 2 sts remain, K2tog.

Row 2 Purl.

Repeat Rows 1 and 2 until 11 sts remain, ending on a purl row.

Next row: (Picot edge) *K2tog, YO, repeat from * across row, ending with K 1.

Row 1 Purl.

Row 2 KFB first st, K until one st remains, KFB.

Repeat rows 1 and 2 until 19 sts remain, ending with a purl row.

ST st for 6 rows, ending with purl row.

Row 1 K2tog on first st, K until 2 sts remain, K2tog.

Row 2 Purl.

Repeat rows 1 and 2 until 7 sts remain.

BO.

Folding at picot edge, right side to right side, sew side seams, leaving bottom of petal open. Invert and dye.

TULIP

TO DYE PETALS

Using a separate bowl and 2 packages for each color, mix Kool-Aid with ⅓ cup tepid water and ⅓ cup white vinegar. Make sure Kool-Aid is thoroughly dissolved.

Soak each petal in bowl with a ratio of ⅔ tepid water to ⅓ white vinegar. While still wet, place each petal on microwaveable dish and, using the red dye, start at the base of the tulip and "paint" upward. (A brush or eyedropper can be used for this process.) Leave a few "streaks" of white as you go. Using yellow dye and starting at the picot edge, paint top edge and into streaks. Be sure and dye both sides of the petal. Set dye by microwaving for 2 minutes on highest power. Immediately rinse in cold running water. Lay flat to dry.

STAMENS (Make 25 for each sock)

Using Color C, cut yarn into 30" lengths. Fold in half and make finger cords. (See page 23)

Dye with yellow dye.

STEMS (Make 5 I-cords for each sock)

Using Color D and DPN, CO 4 sts. Knit 1 row. Do not turn work. Slide sts to opposite end of DPN and K, pulling the yarn snug at the back. Repeat knitting and sliding until each I-cord measures 5½". BO by pulling yarn through all 4 sts. Cut yarn, leaving a 6" tail.

Most hobby stores carry a small hand-cranked machine that helps you make long I-cords quickly. It is a great tool for making the extended lengths needed for this sock.

LEAVES (Make 3 for each sock)

Using Color D and DPNs, CO 26 sts. (8 sts on Needle #1, 9 sts each on Needles #2 and #3.)

Join, being careful not to twist.

Knit until piece measures 2".

Next 2 rounds: *SSK, K until 2 sts remain on the round, K2tog.

Knit 8 rounds.

Repeat from * 4 more times. (6 sts remain). Thread tapestry needle and pull through to bind off.

FINISHING

Using tails, tightly tie 5 "stamens" onto the back side of one petal (which will become the center petal), working the ends of the stamens inside the petal.

Place a second petal halfway on the front of the first (center) petal. Securely stitch in place, going about halfway up the inside center petal.

Place third petal on other side and stitch into place.

Wrap bases of both front petals around the base of center petal and secure.

With a tapestry needle and using double or quadruple strands of Color D, make long stitches at the base of the petals, pulling all three together. This will simulate where the stem joins the flower.

With black embroidery floss, stitch through the extreme ends of each stamen, making several passes. Knot several times and closely trim floss.

Work all ends into stems.

Place one stem in the middle of the base of each leaf and securely sew into place. Fold the leaf over and sew bottom of leaf together. Sew the two sides of the folded leaf up for about an inch. Securely attach the base of the leaf to the top edge of the brown ridge. Attach the tops of each stem to the bottoms of each tulip. Secure stems along side. Position leaves and secure.

GRASS (Make 40 pieces for each sock)

Cut 40 36" lengths of Color D to make the finger cords for the grass.

At the line where the blue changes to brown, evenly distribute the "grass" around the sock, securing it by knotting in place. Work in ends.

Turn the edge and hem.

Work in any loose ends.

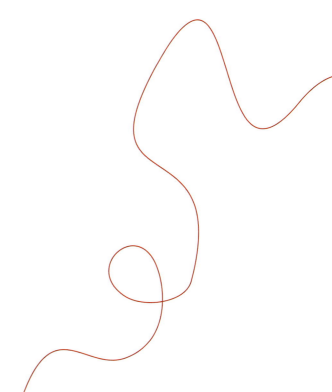

TUBE SOCK

I have always been intrigued with knitting patterns worked in the opposite direction than the usual, like sweaters that start at the cuff of one sleeve and end at the opposite cuff, or scarves that are worked lengthwise instead of widthwise. This sock is my homage to that tradition. No doubt, some will say it is misnamed, as a true tube sock has no heel or shaping. Incorporating a few interesting techniques, like a provisional cast-on, garter stitch grafting, and an attached I-cord trim, this sock is a good one for someone who is ready to explore a new approach to sock knitting.

SIZES	CM: 6" (CL: 7", AS: 8", AM: 9", AL: 10") leg circumference
GAUGE	6 stitches per inch
YARN	DK Weight
	Color A: 1 Skein (200-225 yds) Elsebeth Lavold, Silky Wool, Color 64 (Orange) 45% Wool, 35% Silk, 20% Nylon (50 g, 175M)
	Color B: 1 Skein (200-225 yds) Elsebeth Lavold, Silky Wool, Color 73 (Green) 45% Wool, 35% Silk, 20% Nylon (50 g, 175M)
	Color C: 1 Skein (200-225 yds) Elsebeth Lavold, Silky Wool, Color 85 (Blue) 45% Wool, 35% Silk, 20% Nylon (50 g, 175M)
	Color D: 1 Skein (200-225 yds) Elsebeth Lavold, Silky Wool, Color 69 (Purple) 45% Wool, 35% Silk, 20% Nylon (50 g, 175M)
NEEDLES	Circular or straight size 3 (3.25)
	DPN size 3 (3.25 mm), or size to obtain gauge
NOTIONS	Tapestry needle
	Markers (optional)
	Crochet Hook, Size F (3.75 mm)
	Polyester Fiber Fill (optional)

LEG

The leg of this sock is worked flat on a circular or straight needle, working in an garter stitch (knit every row) of 2 rows each of 2 alternating colors, followed by a section of Rev St St (purl side is the public side). The Rev St St sections will be sewn together to form vertical "tubes" that run up the leg. The finished leg will be joined by a garter stitch grafting.

Using waste yarn, provisionally cast-on (See page 105) 30 (36, 42, 48, 52) sts.

With Color A, K 1 row.

With Color B, K 2 rows.

With Color C, K 2 rows.

Then P a row and K a row for a total of 12 rows, working with Color C and ending with a K row.

*With Color B, K 2 rows.

With Color A, K 2 rows.

Repeat from * 1 (1, 1, 2, 2) more times.

With Color B, K 2 rows.

With Color D: K 2 rows, then P a row and K a row for a total of 12 rows, ending with a K row.

Working in garter stitch for 2 rows of each color, beginning with Color B and alternating with Color A for a total of 12 (12, 12, 14, 14) ending in Color B.

Continue to work these garter stitch/tube sections, alternating the tubes between Color C and Color D until you have a total of 6 sections. End the last section with 10 (10, 10, 12, 12) rows.

Cut both Color A and Color B; however, leave a 20"-24" tail of Color A to use for grafting.

On the WS, sew the two edges of each tube together. (For a bit more drama, you can stuff these tubes with leftover yarn or a small amount of fiberfill.)

Remove the waste yarn of the provisional cast-on, placing the original stitches on another needle.

With Color A, using the Garter Stitch Graft, (See sidebar this page) graft the leg of the sock together:

Color A will be on the front needle and Color B will be on the back needle. (When holding the two needles together, there will be a purl ridge against a purl ridge on the inside.)

Beginning at the base of one of the tubes, with Color A, pick up and K:

48 (56, 64, 72, 80) sts, dividing the sts onto 3 DPNs as follows:

> Needle #1: 12 (14, 16, 18, 20)
> Needle #2: 24 (28, 32, 36, 40)
> Needle #3: 12 (14, 16, 18, 20)

Knit for ½".

HEEL FLAP

Beginning on Needle #3 (RS), *Sl 1 as if to P, K 1, repeat from *, working across needles 3 and 1. You now have a total of 24 (28, 32, 36, 40) sts on each of the 2 needles. (The stitches held on Needle #2 will be worked later for the instep.)

Row 1 Turn work (WS). Sl 1 purlwise, P to end of row.

Row 2 Turn work (RS). *Sl 1 purlwise, K 1, repeat from * across row.

Repeat Rows 1 and 2 for a total of 24 (28, 32, 36, 40) rows, ending with row 1.

GARTER STITCH GRAFTING

Garter Stitch Grafting, like the standard Kitchener Stitch Grafting, is easy once you get the rhythm or routine in your mind and fingers.

Working with the same number of stitches on two needles, hold the needles in the left hand with the purl ridge facing a purl ridge.

1 Thread a tapestry needle and insert into first stitch on the front needle as if to PURL . . . LEAVE this stitch on the needle.

2 Repeat #1 on back needle.

3 Thread yarn through stitch on front needle as if to KNIT and SLIP that stitch off . . . then on the same needle, thread through the next stitch as if to PURL and LEAVE it on the needle.

4 Repeat #3 on back needle.

5 Repeat #3 and #4 until one stitch remains on both the front and back needle. Thread the yarn through the front stitch as if to KNIT and slip off. Repeat on the back needle. Adjust tension to match the tension of the work. Weave in ends.

TURNING THE HEEL (Short Rows)

Row 1 (RS) K 14 (16, 18, 20, 22), SSK, K 1, turn work.

Row 2 (WS) Sl 1 purlwise, P5, P2tog, P 1, turn work.

Row 3 Sl 1 purlwise, K until 1 st before the gap formed on last row, SSK (bringing together the st before and the st after the gap). K 1. Turn work.

Row 4 Sl 1 purlwise, P until 1 st before the gap formed on last row, P2tog (1 st before the gap and 1 st after the gap), P 1. Turn work.

Repeat rows 3 and 4 until all sts have been worked, ending on row 4 (WS). In some sizes the last 2 rows may not have a single stitch to knit or purl, so end those 2 rows with the decrease of SSK or P2tog. You will have 14 (16, 18, 20, 22) sts remaining.

GUSSET

Working on the heel flap, K 7 (8, 9, 10, 11) sts. With a new needle (which will now be needle #1), K 7 (8, 9, 10, 11) sts. On the same needle, pick up 12-14 (14-16, 16-18, 18-20, 20-22) sts along the side of the heel flap.

Work across Needle #2 (the instep stitches that have been waiting patiently). For Needle #3, pick up 12-14 (14-16, 16-18, 18-20, 20-22) sts from the other side of the heel flap, and then K the 7 (8, 9, 10, 11) sts from the heel flap. You should now have (more or less) 20 (23, 26, 29, 32) sts on Needle #1, 24 (28, 32, 36, 40) on Needle #2, and 20 (23, 26, 29, 32) on Needle #3.

Round 1 Needle #1: K until 3 sts remain, K2tog, K 1. Needle #2: K across. Needle #3; K 1, SSK, K to end.

> This first decrease round is a good chance to take care of that extra stitch that you may have picked up along one side of your heel flap. For example, if you have 22 sts on needle #1 and 23 sts on needle #3, do the decrease on needle #1 and omit it on needle #3 for one time only. Thus, you will have an even number of stitches on both sides of your heel flap.

Round 2 Knit.

Repeat Rounds 1 and 2 until you have 12 (14, 16, 18, 20) sts on Needle #1, 24 (28, 32, 36, 40) on Needle #2, and 12 (14, 16, 18, 20) on Needle #3.

> You have shaped your heel and returned to the same number of stitches you cast on.

FOOT

Knit until piece measures 4½" (5½", 6½", 7½", 8") from the back of the heel to the base of the big toe, approximately 3" shorter than the desired finished size.

Change to Color C and K ½".

Change to Color D and K ½".

TOE

Round 1 Needle #1: work until 3 sts remain, K2tog, K 1. Needle #2: K 1, SSK, K until 3 sts remain, K2tog, K 1. Needle #3: K 1, SSK, K to end.

Round 2 Knit.

Repeat Rounds 1 and 2 until 5 (7, 8, 9, 10) sts remain on Needle #1, 10 (14, 16, 18, 20) sts remain on Needle #2, and 5 (7, 8, 9, 10) sts remain on Needle #3.

Then repeat Round 1 until a total of 8 sts remain (4 sts on 2 needles).

Graft these 8 sts by using Kitchener stitch. (See page 41)

FINISHING

Using waste yarn and DPN, provisionally CO 4 sts. Using Color A, K 1 row. Slide sts to the opposite end of the DPN and K 3 sts, slip the next st and pick up and knit 1 st from the edge of the sock leg, beginning at the tube at the back of the sock. Pass the slipped st over this new st. Slide the sts to the opposite end of the needle. Continue to K the first 3 sts, slip 1 and pick up a new one, thus making an I-cord and attaching it at the same time. Once you have encircled the sock, remove the waste yarn and graft these stitches together, using the standard Kitchener stitch. (See page 41)

Work in all ends.

CROCHETED PROVISIONAL CAST-ON

Like most techniques in knitting, there are a number of ways to accomplish a provisional cast-on. After experimenting with many of them, I find the following to be the easiest to both cast on the stitches and then to retrieve the live stitches when needed. Although it is called a crocheted provisional cast-on, it is not to be confused with the method in which one picks up stitches from a chain. In this version, the stitches are placed on the needle with a crochet hook as you cast them on, and then this waste yarn is pulled out when you need the stitches.

1 Using a smooth waste yarn, with the crochet hook in the right hand and the working yarn in the left hand, make a slip knot, followed by 3-4 chain stitches. Holding the needle and the crocheted chain in the left hand, place the working yarn UNDER the needle and the hook on TOP of the needle.

2 * Pick up a stitch with the hook.

3 Throw the yarn back under the needle, thus casting on one stitch on the needle. Repeat from * until the desired number of stitches are on your needle.

NOTE It is important to remember that, when using this cast-on, the first row using your working yarn MUST be either all knit or all purl. Throwing the yarn between stitches on this row will make retrieving the live stitches, when needed, almost impossible.

4 Then make 8-10 chain stitches and pull the yarn through the last stitch. (Note: by making the end chain longer than the first one, you can easily know where to start to unravel the chain when you need the live stitches. It is easy to remember if you relate the "long" chain to a "long-tail" cast-on. Trying to unravel from the shorter end will not work . . . thus the trick for the longer tail.)

5 After you have worked your piece and need to retrieve the live stitches from the provisional cast-on, simply unravel the longer chain, being careful to pick up each stitch as it is freed.

For video instructions please visit:
www.youtube.com/watch?v=wUdM-mHWIAE&feature

TWIST AND SHOUT

Cat Bordhi, the sock designer, author, and my mentor, designed a hat—the Anemone Hat—that overflows with these knitted-in twists. When I asked her if she would share with me how she made the twists, she enthusiastically said yes, explaining that Annie Modesitt, the renowned designer and teacher, had taught her. "Annie taught me," Cat beamed, "and I am teaching you. Now you must teach the world!" I added the loops for more interest. So here it is: Cat's (and Annie's) Twist. Please share this fun technique with all your friends.

TWIST

SIZES	CM:6" (CL:7", AS:8", AM:9", AL:10") leg circumference
GAUGE	5 stitches per inch
YARN	Bulky weight 4 Skeins (400 yds) Nashua Handknits, Vignette, Color NVIG004 Gold Denim 100% Superwash Wool
NEEDLES	DPN size 5 (3.75 mm), or size to obtain gauge
NOTIONS	Tapestry needle Markers (optional)

TO MAKE TWIST (MT)

Work until placement of twist K 1, leaving the original stitch on left needle. Pull a new loop through the stitch, extending to the desired length. (For consistency, I use the length of the DPN plus a couple of inches, approximately 7", resulting in a twist of approximately 3".) Once the loop is extended, twist for desired curl. After trial and error, I determined that 20 twists would result in a curl that's not too loose or too tight. Once the loop is twisted, return its end to the left needle and K2tog (through the replaced loop and the original stitch), thus securing the twisted loop. Adjust the twist if necessary.

TO MAKE LOOP (ML)

Carefully open the end of a previously knitted-in twist and slip onto the left needle. Knit this loop and the next stitch together. Adjust attached loop.

LEG

CO 32 (36, 40, 44, 48) sts, as follows:

Needle #1: 8 (9, 10, 11, 12)
Needle #2: 16 (18 20, 22, 24)
Needle #3: 8 (9, 10, 11, 12)

Join, being careful not to twist.

For a garter stitch edge, (K 1 round, P 1 round) twice. (This will create a slightly rolled edge.)

Round 1 *MT, K 3, repeat from * around.

Rounds 2, 3 Knit.

Round 4 K 3, *MT, K 3, repeat from *around, ending with MT.

Round 5 K 3, *ML, K 3, repeat from *around, ending with ML.

Round 6 Knit.

Repeat rounds 1-6 until piece measures 4½" (5½", 6½", 7½", 8½").

Knit for 1" more, ending with the last st on Needle #2.

HEEL FLAP

Beginning on needle #3 (RS), *Sl 1 purlwise, K 1, repeat from *, working across needles 3 and 1. You now have a total of 16 (18, 20, 24, 26) sts on each of the 2 needles. (The stitches held on needle #2 will be worked later for the instep.)

Row 1 Turn work (WS). Sl 1 purlwise, P to end of row.

Row 2 Turn work (RS). *Sl 1 purlwise, K 1, repeat from * across row.

Repeat Rows 1 and 2 for a total of 16 (18, 20, 24, 26) rows, ending with row 1.

TURNING THE HEEL (Short Rows)

Row 1 (RS) Knit 10 (11, 12, 13, 14), SSK, K 1, turn work.

Row 2 (WS) Sl 1 purlwise, P 5, P2tog, P 1, turn work.

Row 3 Sl 1 purlwise, K until 1 st before the gap formed on last row, SSK (bringing together the st before and the st after the gap), K 1. Turn work.

Row 4 Sl 1 purlwise, P until 1 st before the gap formed on last row, P2tog (1 st before the gap and 1 st after the gap), P 1. Turn work.

Repeat rows 3 and 4 until all sts have been worked, ending on row 4 (WS). In some sizes the last 2 rows may not have a single stitch to knit or purl, so end those 2 rows with the decrease of SSK or P2tog. You will have 10 (12, 12, 14, 14) sts remaining.

TWISTS

1 Knit into the stitch where you want to place the twist, and leave the original stitch on the left needle. Extend the loop of the new loop. If you want to make all the twists in your work the same size, note the length of your extended loop and maintain that length for each loop.

2 Twist the loop around your finger, noting the number of twists for consistency.

3 Once the twist is tight on your right finger, return the end of the loop back to the left needle. The twist will wind on itself and may need a bit of untangling.

4 Knit the returned loop and the original stitch together, thus anchoring the twist.

5 To make a TWISTED LOOP, on the next knit row, work until the stitch of the twist below. Place the end of the twist on the left needle and knit it together with the original stitch, thus creating a twisted loop.

For video instructions please visit:
www.youtube.com/watch?v=Ad8tU3HP7kQ

GUSSET

Working on the heel flap, K 5 (6, 6, 7, 7) sts. With a new needle (which becomes needle #1), K 5 (6, 6, 7, 7) sts. On the same needle, pick up 8-10 (9-11, 10-12, 11-13, 12-14) sts along the side of the heel flap

Work across needle #2 (the instep stitches that have been waiting patiently). For needle #3, pick up 8-10 (9-11, 10-12, 11-13, 12-14) sts from the other side of the heel flap and then K the 5 (6, 6, 7, 7) sts from the heel flap. You should now have (more or less) 14 (16, 17, 19, 20) on needle #1, 16 (18, 20, 24, 26) sts on needle #2, and 14 (16, 17, 19, 20) on needle #3.

Round 1

> Needle #1: K until 3 sts remain, K2tog, K 1.
> Needle #2: K across.
> Needle #3: K 1, SSK, K to end.

....

This first decrease round is a good chance to take of that extra stitch that you may have picked up along one side of your heel flap. For example, if you have 18 sts on needle #1 and 17 sts on needle #3, do the decrease on needle #1 and omit it on needle #3 for one round only. Then you will have an equal number of stitches on both sides of your heel flap.)

....

Round 2 Knit.

Repeat Rows 1 and 2 until you have 8 (9, 10, 11, 12) sts on needle #1, 16 (18, 20, 22, 24) on needle #2, and 8 (9, 10, 11, 12) on needle #3.

....

You have shaped your heel and returned to the same number of stitches you cast on.

....

FOOT

Work until piece measures 5½" (6½", 7½", 8½", 9") from back of heel to the base of the big toe, approximately 2" shorter than the desired finished size.

TOE

Round 1 On Needle #1: work until 3 sts remain, K2tog, K 1. Needle #2: K 1, SSK, K until 3 sts remain, K2tog, K 1. Needle #3: K 1, SSK, K to end.

Round 2 Knit.

Repeat Rounds 1 and 2 until 5 (7, 8, 9, 10) sts remain on needle #1, 10 (14, 16, 18, 20) sts on needle #2, and 5 (7, 8, 9, 10) sts on needle #3.

Then repeat Round 1 until a total of 8 sts remain (4 sts on 2 needles).

Graft these 8 sts by using Kitchener stitch. (Page 47)

FINISHING

Work in all loose ends.

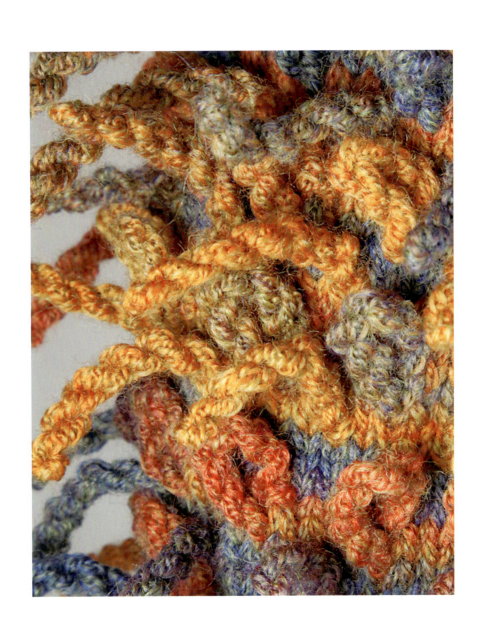

VARSITY

What could be more classic than a ribbed sock with a few simple stripes . . . a sock you might wear to the Friday night ball game. Add some I-cords around the ankle and you have a sock definitely ready for the A team. Move the I-cords up the leg and you have yet another look. Or consider working the stripes in reverse stockinette stitch for even more interest and texture. The knitted-in I-cords in make the inside of the sock just as neatly finished as the outside. Go team!

SIZES CM: 6" (CL: 7", AS: 8", AM: 9", AL: 10") leg circumference

GAUGE 8 stitches per inch

YARN Fingering Weight
Color A: 1 Skein (400-425 yds) Berroco, Ultra Alpaca Fine, #1201 Winter White
50% Peruvian Wool, 20% Super Fine Alpaca, 30% Nylon
Color B: 25 yards Berroco, Ultra Alpaca Fine, Color #1285 Oceanic Mix
50% Peruvian Wool, 20% Super Fine Alpaca, 30% Nylon
Color C: 25 yards Berroco, Ultra Alpaca Fine, Color #127 Pea Soup Mix
50% Peruvian Wool, 20% Super Fine Alpaca, 30% Nylon
Color D: 40 yards Berroco, Sox, Color #1441 Fergus
75% Superwash Wool, 25% Nylon

NEEDLES DPN size 1 (2.25 mm), or size to obtain gauge

NOTIONS Tapestry needle
Markers (optional)
64 coilless safety pins or small stitch holders

LEG

Using Color A, CO 48 (56, 64, 72, 80) sts, distributed onto DPNs as follows:

Needle #1: 12 (14, 16, 18, 20)
Needle #2: 24 (28, 32, 36, 40)
Needle #3: 12 (14, 16, 18, 20)

Join, being careful not to twist.

*K2, P2. Repeat from * around.

Continue until piece measures 2".

Continuing with color A, K 4 (5, 6, 7, 8) rounds.

Change to color B, and K for 4 (5, 6, 7, 8) rounds.

. . . .
To avoid a horizontal stripe "jog" on this and all subsequent color changes, K the first round in the new color. Slip the first st of the second round, then knit following rounds normally.
. . . .

Change to color A, K 4 (5, 6, 7, 8) rounds.

Change to color C, K 4 (5, 6, 7, 8) rounds.

Change to color A, K for ½" (1", 1½", 2", 2½") inches.

Change to color C, K for 4 (5, 6, 7, 8) rounds.

Change to color D and K for 2 rounds. Next round, *K2, slip next 2 sts onto a safety pin or stitch holder, then, using the backward loop method, CO 2. Repeat from * around. (See page 29)

Knit 2 rounds.

Next round: * slip next 2 sts onto a safety pin or stitch holder, CO 2, K2. repeat from * around.

. . . .
The first I-cord round began with K 2. This one does not, thus alternating the spacing of the completed I-cords.
. . . .

Knit 2 rounds, for a total of 8 rounds in color D.

Change to color B, K4 (5, 6, 7, 8) rounds.

Change to color A, K4 (5, 6, 7, 8) rounds.

114 THE EMBELLISHED SOCK

HEEL FLAP

Beginning on needle #3 (RS), *Sl 1 as if to P, K 1, repeat from *, working across needles 3 and 1. You now have a total of 24 (28, 32, 36, 40) sts on each of the 2 needles. (The stitches held on needle #2 will be worked later for the instep.)

Row 1 Turn work (WS). Sl 1 purlwise, P to end of row.

Row 2 Turn work (RS). *Sl 1 purlwise, K 1, repeat from * across row.

Repeat Rows 1 and 2 for a total of 24 (28, 32, 36, 40) rows, ending with row 1.

TURNING THE HEEL (Short Rows)

Row 1 (RS) K 14 (16, 18, 20, 22), SSK, K 1, turn work.

Row 2 (WS) Sl 1 purlwise, P5, P2tog, P 1, turn work.

Row 3 Sl 1 purlwise, K until 1 st before the gap formed on last row, SSK (bringing together the st before and the st after the gap). K 1. Turn work.

Row 4 Sl 1 purlwise, P until 1 st before the gap formed on last row, P2tog (1 st before the gap and 1 st after the gap), P 1. Turn work.

Repeat rows 3 and 4 until all sts have been worked, ending on row 4 (WS). In some sizes the last 2 rows may not have a single stitch to knit or purl, so end those 2 rows with the decrease of SSK or P2tog. You will have 14 (16, 18, 20, 22) sts remaining.

BE CREATIVE

Who says a certain embellishment has to be located on a sock exactly where the pattern calls for it? It's fun to experiment with the placement of such details. One time put it at the cuff, the next time at the ankle, and the next time at both the cuff and ankle. Be creative. What about making the location of a detail on one sock in one place and in another place on the companion sock?

GUSSET

Working on the heel flap, K 7 (8, 9, 10, 11) sts. With a new needle (which becomes needle #1), K 7 (8, 9, 10, 11) sts. On the same needle, pick up 12-14 (14-16, 16-18, 18-20, 20-22) sts along the side of the heel flap.

Work across needle #2 (the instep stitches that have been waiting patiently). For needle #3, pick up 12-14 (14-16, 16-18, 18-20, 20-22) sts from the other side of the heel flap, and then K the 7 (8, 9, 10, 11) sts from the heel flap. You should now have (more or less) 20 (23, 26, 29, 32) on needle #1, 24 (28, 32, 36, 40) sts on needle #2, and 20 (23, 26, 29, 32) on needle #3.

Round 1 Needle #1: K until 3 sts remain, K2tog, K 1. Needle #2: K across. Needle #3: K 1, SSK, K to end.

> This first decrease round is a good chance to take care of that extra stitch that you may have picked up along one side of your heel flap. For example, if you have 22 sts on needle #1 and 23 sts on needle #3, do the decrease on needle #1 and omit it on needle #3 for one time only. Thus, you will have an even number of stitches on both sides of your heel flap.

Round 2 Knit.

Repeat Rounds 1 and 2 until you have 12 (14, 16, 18, 20) sts on needle #1, 24 (28, 32, 36, 40) on needle #2, and 12 (14, 16, 18, 20) on needle #3.

> You have shaped your heel and returned to the same number of stitches you cast on.

FOOT

Knit until piece measures 4" (4¾", 5½", 5¾", 6") from the back of the heel.

Change to color C, K for 4 (5, 6, 7, 8) rounds.

Change to color A, K for 4 (5, 6, 7, 8) rounds.

Change to color B, K for 4 (5, 6, 7, 8) rounds.

Change to color A, K for 4 (5, 6, 7, 8) rounds.

TOE

Round 1 Needle #1: work until 3 sts remain, K2tog, K 1. Needle #2: K 1, SSK, K until 3 sts remain, K2tog, K 1. Needle #3: K 1, SSK, K to end.

Round 2 Knit.

Repeat Rounds 1 and 2 until 5 (7, 8, 9, 10) sts remain on needle #1, 10 (14, 16, 18, 20) sts on needle #2, and 5 (7, 8, 9, 10) sts on needle #3.

Then repeat Round 1 until a total of 8 sts remain (4 sts on 2 needles).

Graft these 8 sts by using Kitchener stitch. (See page 41)

FINISHING

Knitted-in I-cords: Working from the top of the sock down, slip 2 sts from one of the safety pins or stitch holders onto a DPN. Then pick up 1 st from the left-hand "V" on the left side of the CO sts and 1 st from the right-hand "V" on the right side, for a total of 4 sts on the needle. Using color D yarn and leaving a 6" tail, K one row. Slide sts to the other end of the DPN and K across again. Continue knitting a row and sliding the work to the opposite end of the needle, making an I-cord. Knit until the I-cord measures 1¼". Leaving a 6" tail, cut yarn, thread through sts, and work in the loose end. At the base of the I-cord, thread a tapestry needle, tighten up I-cord, and work in the end into the I-cord itself. Repeat for each stitch holder. (See page 29)

Work in all loose ends.

WINTER WONDERLAND

Knitting with beads has long fascinated me, and at the same time discouraged me. The idea of threading all those beads on my yarn one by one, hoping and praying that I got them in the correct order, just seemed too tedious. Thus I never pursued intricate patterns that called for beads. All that changed when on a lucky visit to a local yarn shop in Maine, the enthusiastic shop owner displayed a beautifully detailed garment scattered throughout with small pearls and beads knitted in very complicated patterns. "How in the world," I asked, "did one ever get all those beads on the yarn in the exact order and then work the pattern so beautifully?" She explained how one bead at a time can be added, using a crochet hook, allowing the knitter to follow any chart and make any pattern without the drudgery of threading all those beads on the yarn beforehand! What a simple technique that has made me love knitting with beads. I think you will enjoy the technique too . . . happy beading!

SIZES	CM:6" (CL:7", AS:8", AM:9", AL:10") leg circumference
GAUGE	8 stitches per inch

YARN	Fingering Weight
	For socks:
	    (MC) 1 Skein (400-425 yds) Berroco, Ultra Alpaca Fine, #1201 Winter White
	        50% Peruvian Wool, 20% Super Fine Alpaca, 30% Nylon
	    (CC) 2 Skeins (400-425 yds) Rowan, Kidsilk Haze, #634 Cream, held double
	        70% Super Kid Mohair, 30% Silk
	Waste yarn for provisional cast-on (optional)

NEEDLES	DPN size 1 (2.25 mm), or size to obtain gauge
NOTIONS	Tapestry needle Markers (optional) 100 grams size 6 Silver Lined Clear AB Round Japanese Seed Beads 30 grams size 6 Opaque White Luster Round Japanese Seed Beads Size 12 (1.00 mm) Crochet Hook Size C (2.75 mm) crochet hook for provisional cast-on (optional)

LEG

For the entire sock, K 10 (12, 13, 14, 16) rounds of MC and then 10 (12, 13, 14, 16) rounds of CC (held double) for alternating stripes. At each color change, remember to slip the first stitch to avoid the "jog." The heel flap, short rows, and toe will be worked in MC.

For the edge of this sock you have two options: a knitted-in hem where you use a Provisional Cast-On, or a Turned Edge where you do a regular cast-on and hem when finished.

Provisional Cast-On (See page 105): Using waste yarn, CO 48 (56, 64, 72, 80) sts, distributed onto DPNs as follows:

    Needle #1: 12 (14, 16, 18, 20)
    Needle #2: 24 (28, 32, 36, 40)
    Needle #3: 12 (14, 16, 18, 20)

Join, being careful not to twist.

Using MC, K 8 rounds, P 1 round, K 8 rounds, remove the waste yarn, place the stitches on DPNs and then, using a third needle, k2tog, taking 1 st from the front needle and 1 st from the back needle. Thus, you will have a neat "finished" hem. Note: If you choose this option the beading will begin on the next round and the top edge of your sock will be 4 rounds longer than shown in the photograph. (See page 123)

Turned Edge: Using MC, CO 48 (56, 64, 72, 80) sts, distributed onto DPNs as follows:

    Needle #1: 12 (14, 16, 18, 20)
    Needle #2: 24 (28, 32, 36, 40)
    Needle #3: 12 (14, 16, 18, 20)

Join, being careful not to twist.

Knit 8 rounds. (These rounds will be turned to form a hem during the finishing process.)

Next round: Purl. (This round makes the turning of the hem cleaner and easier.)

Continuing using MC, K 4 rounds. Then begin to work the bead chart in 8 st repeats around. (See page 123). Working in alternating stripes, work the bead chart in 8-st repeats around. To add beads, work until the st before the bead st on the chart. Place the bead on the crochet hook. Pull the charted stitch from the left needle through the bead. Replace the stitch on the left needle and knit as usual, anchoring the bead.

After 6 (8, 9, 10, 12) rounds of beading, change to CC (held double) and continue to work in alternating stripes of 10 (12, 13, 14, 16) rounds of each yarn.

Work for a total of 6 stripes. The piece will measure approximately 6 (6½", 7", 8", 9") from the purl edge. End with the last st on needle #2.

HEEL FLAP

Change to MC. Beginning on needle #3 (RS), *Sl 1 as if to P, K 1, repeat from *, working across needles 3 and 1. You now have a total of 24 (28, 32, 36, 40) sts on each of the 2 needles. (The stitches held on needle #2 will be worked later for the instep.)

Row 1 Turn work (WS). Sl 1 purlwise, P to end of row.

Row 2 Turn work (RS). *Sl 1 purlwise, K 1, repeat from * across row.

Repeat Rows 1 and 2 for a total of 24 (28, 32, 36, 40) rows, ending with row 1.

TURNING THE HEEL (Short Rows)

Row 1 (RS) K 14 (16, 18, 20, 22), SSK, K 1, turn work.

Row 2 (WS) Sl 1 purlwise, P5, P2tog, P 1, turn work.

Row 3 Sl 1 purlwise, K until 1 st before the gap formed on last row, SSK (bringing together the st before and the st after the gap). K 1. Turn work.

Row 4 Sl 1 purlwise, P until 1 st before the gap formed on last row, P2tog (1 st before the gap and 1 st after the gap), P 1. Turn work.

Repeat rows 3 and 4 until all sts have been worked, ending on row 4 (WS). In some sizes the last 2 rows may not have a single stitch to knit or purl, so end those 2 rows with the decrease of SSK or P2tog. You will have 14 (16, 18, 20, 22) sts remaining.

GUSSET

Continuing with MC and working on the heel flap, K 7 (8, 9, 10, 11) sts. With a new needle (which will now be needle #1), K 7 (8, 9, 10, 11) sts. On the same needle, pick up 12-14 (14-16, 16-18, 18-20, 20-22) sts along the side of the heel flap.

Work across needle #2 (the instep stitches that have been waiting patiently). For needle #3, pick up 12-14 (14-16, 16-18, 18-20, 20-22) sts from the other side of the heel flap, and then K the 7 (8, 9, 10, 11) sts from the heel flap. You should now have (more or less) 20 (23, 26, 29, 32) on needle #1, 24 (28, 32, 36, 40) sts on needle #2, and 20 (23, 26, 29, 32) on needle #3.

Round 1 Needle #1: K until 3 sts remain, K2tog, K 1. Needle #2: K across. Needle #3: K 1, SSK, K to end.

. . . .

This first decrease round is a good chance to take care of that extra stitch that you may have picked up along one side of your heel flap. For example, if you have 22 sts on needle #1 and 23 sts on needle #3, do the decrease on needle #1 and omit it on needle #3 for one time only. Thus, you will have an even number of stitches on both sides of your heel flap.

. . . .

Round 2 Knit.

Repeat Rounds 1 and 2 until you have 12 (14, 16, 18, 20) sts on needle #1, 24 (28, 32, 36, 40) on needle #2, and 12 (14, 16, 18, 20) on needle #3.

. . . .

You have shaped your heel and returned to the same number of stitches you cast on.

. . . .

FOOT

Working with established stripe pattern, after 6 stripes your sock will measure approximately 6 (6½", 7", 8", 9"), from the back of the heel to the base of the big toe, approximately 2" shorter than the desired finished size.

TOE

Change to MC.

Round 1 Needle #1: work until 3 sts remain, K2tog, K 1. Needle #2: K 1, SSK, K until 3 sts remain, K2tog, K 1. Needle #3: K 1, SSK, K to end.

Round 2 Knit.

Repeat Rounds 1 and 2 until 5 (7, 8, 9, 10) sts remain on needle #1, 10 (14, 16, 18, 20) sts on needle #2, and 5 (7, 8, 9, 10) sts on needle #3.

Then repeat Round 1 until a total of 8 sts remain (4 sts on 2 needles).

Graft these 8 sts by using Kitchener stitch. (See page 41)

FINISHING

If you chose the Turned Edge option for the sock top, turn at the picot edge and hem carefully.

Work in any loose ends.

EASY BEADING

To add beads, work until the st before the bead st on the chart. Place the bead on the crochet hook. Pull the charted stitch from the left needle through the bead. Replace the stitch on the left needle and knit as usual, anchoring the bead.

For video instructions please visit:
www.youtube.com/watch?v=qADHpPOKBuo

Pearl P

Bead B

repeat section |

ABBREVIATIONS

AS	Adult Small
AL	Adult Large
AM	Adult Medium
BO	Bind Off
CC	Contrasting color
CL	Child Large
CM	Child Medium
CO	Cast On
Dec	Decrease
DPN	Double Point Needle
Inc	Increase
PM	Place Marker
P2tog	Purl 2 together
Rev St St	Reverse Stockinette
Rem	Remaining
RS	Right Side
Sl	Slip
K	Knit
K2tog	Knit 2 together
KFB	Knit in the front and back of the same stitch
M1	Make one (increase)
MB	Make Bobble
MC	Main Color
ML	Make Loop
mm	Millimeter
MT	Make Twist
P	Purl
SSK	Slip, slip, knit 2 together
St(s)	Stitch(es)
St St	Stockinette Stitch
WS	Wrong Side
YO	Yarn Over

RESOURCES

Specified yarns may be substituted for any that allows you to obtain the specified gauge.

BERROCO
www.berroco.com

BLUE MOON FIBER ARTS
www.bluemoonfiberarts.com

CASCADE
www.cascadeyarns.com

CHERRY TREE HILL
www.cherryyarn.com

ELSEBETH LAVOLD
www.knittingfever.com

FUSION BEADS
www.fusionbeads.com

KERTZER
www.kertzer.com

NASHUA HANDKNITS
www.nashuahandknits.com

NORO
www.knittingfever.com

REGIA
www.westminsterfibers.com

ROWAN
www.knitrowan.com

SOXX APPEAL
www.knitonecrochettoo.com/soxxappeal.htm

SPUD AND CHLOE
www.spudandchloe.com

SUBLIME
www.knittingfever.com

SWTC INC
www.soysilk.com

TY-DY SOCKS
www.knitonecrochettoo.com/tydysocks.htm

INDEX

Attaching embellishments 34
Beading 123
Bobbles 44, 47, 68
Coilless safety pins 40
Finger cords 23
Grafting
   Garter stitch 103
   Kitchener stitch 41
Heel flaps 59
Hems
   Knitted-in 52
I-cords
   Attaching 65
   Knitted-in 29
   Made easy 64
Jogless stripes 58
Kitchener stitch grafting 41
Kool-Aid dyeing 98
Picking up stitches
   Gusset 97
   Ladder 75
Pompoms 35
Provisional cast-on 105
Ruffles 14
Self-striping yarn 28
Tabi toes 82
Three-needle attachment 15
Twists 109

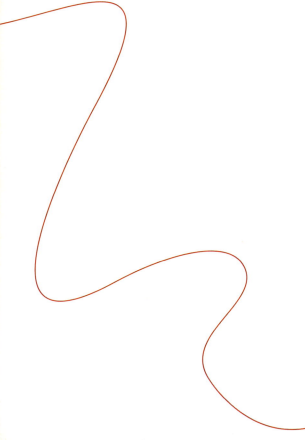

ACKNOWLEDGMENTS

Any project or endeavor can never be accomplished alone. This book is certainly no exception. Heartfelt thanks to:

Knitter's Magazine, XRX, Inc., and the yarn manufacturers for their sponsorship of the "Think Outside the Sox" contest that started me on my journey of making creative—some would say outlandish—socks. Thank you, judges, **Cat Bordhi**, **Sandi Rosner**, and **Lucy Neatby**.

Cat Bordhi, my friend and my mentor. Her invitation to become one of her "visionaries" gave me the extra confidence needed to see my dreams fulfilled. Cat is one of those generous people who truly care about the knitting community. Her enthusiasm and giving spirit are contagious and will forever serve as a role model for me as I continue on my knitting career.

The Sunday Afternoon Knitters at Grapes & Beans in Clayton, Georgia, who epitomize the congeniality among knitters.

The many students in my workshops, whose patient understanding helped me muddle my way through my early patterns. Your positive feedback, constructive criticism, and overall enthusiasm for my work have made this book so much better.

Ava Navin, my technical editor, thank you. Ava harnessed my wordiness, corrected my errors (we hope!), and caught my omissions (we hope!). This arduous task was accomplished with great patience and excitement.

Burtch Hunter, my book designer, who from the beginning understood and championed my vision for the book, making it more beautiful and useful than I could ever have imagined.

Silver Threads & Golden Needles in Franklin, North Carolina. Thank you, Kristen McDougall, Virginia Murphy, and Amy Murphy.

Strings & Stitches Yarn Shoppe in Ellijay, Georgia. Thank you, Karen Moss and Janice Moss.

Bumbleberry Yarn and Gifts in Clarksville, Georgia. Thank you, Bonnie Walsh.

Sean Riley for his beautiful charts.

Peter McIntosh for your beautiful photography.

Indeed, no one accomplishes much alone. Thanks to all for your help and support.

The Embellished Sock